LEGENDS
OF THE TOUR

THE HOTTEST, TOUGHEST AND FASTEST RIDERS OF THIS DECADE

LEGENDS
OF THE TOUR

THE HOTTEST, TOUGHEST AND FASTEST RIDERS OF THIS DECADE

ELLIS BACON, DANIEL FRIEBE, ALEX HINDS,
REECE HOMFRAY, JONATHAN LOVELOCK, FELIX LOWE, ANTHONY TAN

hardie grant books
MELBOURNE · LONDON

CONTENTS

FOREWORD by Phil Liggett

JÉRÉMY ROY   RUI COSTA   ADAM HANSEN   JENS VOIGT   THOMAS VOECKLER

ANDY SCHLECK   CADEL EVANS   BRADLEY WIGGINS   CHRIS FROOME   VINCENZO NIBALI

ALEJANDRO VALVERDE   PIERRE ROLLAND   SAMUEL SÁNCHEZ   CHRISTOPHE RIBLON   JURGEN VAN DEN BROECK

SKY   ORICA-GREENEDGE   MOVISTAR   TINKOFF-SAXO   ASTANA

MARK CAVENDISH   PETER SAGAN   MARCEL KITTEL   ANDRE GREIPEL   ALESSANDRO PETACCHI

FOREWORD

Having covered every Tour de France since 1973, I waited a long time to call my first Australian and British winners. It was touch and go whether I would still be around for the greatest moments of my career!

This beautiful book brings the Tour history up to date, but from an interesting and different perspective, as the riders who often make the winners look as good as they are, get their deserved mention as the real heroes behind the champions.

The Tour's final accolade, of course, goes to the individual winner—a man of extreme talent, who has survived the most rigorous three weeks of his life. They are exceptional men with lungs we can only dream of, and a mental outlook that refuses to recognise defeat.

But to make these men like Alberto Contador, Cadel Evans, Chris Froome, Bradley Wiggins and Vincenzo Nibali look so special, they need a team of talented riders behind them. These people are so often their legs, inspiration and mentors when the going gets tough.

The Tour de France is not just about the final champion in Paris, but about those who make him such along the way. The breakaway specialists, the climbers and the sprinters, are all winning their own Tour de France in the shadow of the one champion who rides proudly onto the Champs Elysees.

Every professional cyclist wants his chance to ride the greatest race of all. Those who can say they did when they are asked are immediately revered as athletes who achieved something very special.

Australians ten years ago began a journey with the Tour that pinnacled with the Cadel Evans victory in 2011. Now it is time for the next phase to begin. This book brings you right up to date with an understanding of La Grande Boucle like never before.

— Phil Liggett
Hertford, UK

Breakaways: They are long, hard, usually fruitless, mostly thankless endeavours, and generally leave riders deprived of energy for days afterwards. So in the middle of the longest, hardest and most important race of the year, why would any rider dare take on such a feat? And who, of these ambitious crusaders, has made an art of riding the breakaway?

Breaks can go on flat, undulating or mountainous stages and they can occur at any point during the race. However, for us fans tuning in to Tour de France coverage, we usually join mid-race when the break is established, and one team is riding a steady tempo at the front. This means that we have missed what is generally an exhilarating flurry of attacks early in the piece.

At the start of any Tour de France stage the formula is the same: the attacks start as soon as the flag drops, and sometime within the first hour the break will form. Whichever team is holding the yellow jersey — and has responsibility for riding the front — will then call for a 'nature break'. All the teams will load up on food and drink, negotiate who else will help set the pace, and then the chase begins. It is a rule of cycling that the break only ever wins if the peloton lets you. Either the sprint teams stuffed it up on a flat stage, or the team leading GC actually wanted a break to go away on a hilly stage. But it is this rather hopeless nature that makes breakaways such honourable exploits.

As a rider in the break, you're hungry, you're thirsty, your back hurts and you've probably got a saddle sore by now. And you are doing this all in the hope that this stage is the one where the big teams mess up. It is this small chance at glory that fuels every pedal stroke.

Jérémy Roy (FDJ), Rui Costa (Lampre-Merida), Jens Voigt (Trek Factory Racing — retired 2014), Adam Hansen (Lotto Soudal) and Thomas Voeckler (Europcar) are five of the best breakaway riders of recent times, all spurred on by the slim possibility of triumph that each breakaway offers. A great breakaway rider can attack a lot, and almost never win, or he can attack few times, but convert those few attacks consistently. Above all, the two elements common to all great breakaway riders are the ability to endure suffering, and the willingness to take a risk. And it's the combination of those elements that make the best breakaways so entertaining for us, the fans.

FIVE GREAT
BREAKAWAY SPECIALISTS

JÉRÉMY ROY

RUI COSTA

ADAM HANSEN

JENS VOIGT

THOMAS VOECKLER

JONATHAN LOVELOCK

JÉRÉMY
ROY

JÉRÉMY ROY HAS RACED every Tour de France from 2010 to 2014 with French team FDJ (previously Francaise de Jeux). It should come as no shock that a French rider, on a French team, is one of the best breakaway riders in the world. Amateur racing in France is regarded as the most aggressive there is, with non-stop breakaway attempts the norm, and Roy upholds this reputation grandly.

In the 2011 Tour de France Roy spent nearly 700km—essentially a third of the race—off the front of the peloton. He was awarded the *dossard rouge*, or red number, for the most aggressive rider on the Stages 4 and 13, and the overall most aggressive for the Tour. Roy spent so much time off the front collecting dribs and drabs from the mid-stage sprint points that he finished eleventh in the Green Jersey competition with 104 points, ahead of many actual sprinters.

Roy turned professional with FDJ back in 2004 and continued studying mechanical and automated engineering for the first three years of his career. In parallel, his cycling education required him to finish three Vueltas a España before he was deemed eligible to race the Tour. In 2008 FDJ Directeur Sportif Marc Madiot deemed Roy ready for the demands of the Tour, he raced—and finished—his first that year and has finished every Tour since.

There are many reasons for riders or teams to want to get in a breakaway, for Jérémy Roy and FDJ, their reasons are twofold. Firstly, they want to get out in front so that when TV coverage starts, their sponsor gets maximum airtime. The riders are literally moving billboards, and the Tour de France is the biggest annual sporting event in the world. With the average WorldTour Team budget hovering around 20 million euros, riders and managers will do whatever they can to keep the sponsors happy.

Secondly, FDJ do not have a sprinter capable of winning a bunch sprint. In 2013 they had Nacer Bouhanni, but every other year from 2010 till now, their best shot of winning a stage was to roll their dice in the early break. And that's exactly what Jérémy Roy does best.

Roy is one of the best breakaway riders because he can *actually* get in a break. If this analysis sounds slightly inane, remember that we don't see on TV the sheer number of attacks launched just to establish a breakaway, we tend to underestimate the difficulty in simply getting there in the first place. Some riders try to go with every attack such that they have maximum chance of being in the break that eventually sticks. Or, they can save their attacks and wait patiently, hoping that they pick the one successful break. Owing to his French aggression, Roy belongs to the former group, and owing to his stamina and persistence, he is never so fatigued that he misses the crucial split.

On Stage 11 of the 2011 Tour de France, a mountainous 156km from Pau to Lourdes, Roy initiated an early break of ten riders that included then world champion Thor Hushovd (Team Garmin-Cervélo). Spending nearly the entire stage off the front with Geraint Thomas (Sky Procycling) the day before was clearly no limiter as Roy set about decimating the breakaway as they climbed the Col d'Aubisque. Roy took off from the group, passed Hushovd who had attacked earlier, and went about establishing a healthy lead.

With 33km of mostly downhill riding to come, and just Hushovd and David Moncoutie (Cofidis) chasing; Roy could almost taste that elusive stage win. It was, however, the strength of the duo behind, and the force of the headwind in front, that thwarted his chances. With 20km to go he held a 1:08 lead, at 10km it was just 18 seconds. With 3km to go it was Hushovd, who by this stage was doing all of the pace setting, who blasted across the gap. Hushovd caught and passed Roy to claim the stage in what was one of the most heartbreaking moments professional cycling has witnessed. Both Hushovd and Moncoutie agreed that Roy's courageous attack was deserving of a stage win.

Roy, fighting back tears, told reporters at the finish line that third place, and the award of most aggressive, was not consolation.

'My creed is to go for it. I'm not a champion, I can't play with the big guns at the summit of the climbs, so I have to out-manoeuvre the peloton with the limited physical capacities I've got,' said Roy at the time. 'I've failed again today. It's infuriating to fail so close to the end.'

But did this failure deter Roy? Certainly not. It only fuelled his aggression, which fuels our viewing pleasure. Roy can and will be seen dangling off the front of the peloton for many Tours de France to come. And the race is better off for it.

LEADING AN ESCAPE ON STAGE 13 OF THE 2011 TOUR

EARLIER, ON STAGE 1

RUI
COSTA

IF JÉRÉMY ROY PAINTS A PICTURE of all-out aggression, Lampre-Merida's Rui Costa presents a vastly different canvas. Costa is calm, calculating and very often victorious. Costa is also a fan favourite having received for the last two years running the most fan mail of any rider at the Tour. Whether it's because he made history in 2013 becoming Portugal's first ever world champion on the road, or it's the three Tour de France stage victories he claimed between 2011 and 2013, he is never far from the headlines.

Just as Roy is the rider who will blast off the front of the peloton and create a breakaway, Costa is the type of rider who waits for a strong break to be established, then scurries across the gap at the last possible minute. In Stage 8 of the 2011 Tour de France, a gruelling 190km from Aigurande to Super-Besse Sancy, Costa (then Movistar) rode across to an already established group of eight riders who were never seen again.

It's another rule of cycling that a breakaway group is only as strong as its weakest rider, the point being, for a rider such as Costa in a group of eight, it serves no purpose for him to ride the strongest turns on the front. When rotating turns, if a rider smashes over the top of whoever was on the front before, he simply makes it devastatingly hard for that rider to get back into the slipstream at the back of the group. Similarly, it serves little purpose to lay out all of your energy to keep a group away, if you have nothing left when it comes time to race for the win amongst the break.

Therefore it's a judgement call each rider has to make: work too hard and the break will stay away, but you will get defeated by your companions;

WINNING STAGE 19 OF THE 2013 TOUR

or, don't work enough and you may be fresh enough to beat your companions, but the peloton will catch you because you didn't get enough of a gap. And it's this ongoing calculation of effort, risk and reward that Costa is so good at making.

On the final ramps of the climb up to Super-Besse in 2011, Costa saved enough energy to blow apart the breakaway and hold on to win the stage just 12 seconds ahead of Philippe Gilbert (Omega Pharma-Lotto) who was closing fast from an aggressive peloton.

When talking to *Bicycling* magazine Costa revealed that he first fell in love with cycling at the age of 11 when his dad bought a 'gorgeous' red bike. Sensing his son's enthusiasm, Manuel Costa set Rui a challenge: if he won the series of junior cycling races around their home in Porto, he would give him the bike.

Costa won those races. He won that bike. And that winning mentality is what makes him a superb breakaway rider.

Following his 2011 stage win, Costa put his calculating mind to good use and chalked up another two excellent breakaway victories in the 2013 Tour de France. In Stage 16, another 168 hilly kilometres from Vaison-la-Romaine to Gap, Costa snuck away in a large group of nearly 40 riders (including fellow breakaway specialists Adam Hansen and

Thomas Voeckler) and was given the green light by the peloton to escape.

In a familiar balance of commitment and preservation, Costa flew past the remainder of the break up the final climb, the 9.5km Col de Manse, and deftly navigated the final descent to seal a comfortable 42-second victory. Often the Tour de France race committee awards the *dossard rouge* for most aggressive to a rider who did not win, but raced with considerable panache. But Costa's Stage 16 victory was so brilliant that he left as stage winner and most aggressive.

Only three days later, Costa struck again, this time slipping into another large group on the hilly Stage 19 from Bourg d'Oisans to Le Grand Bornand. Costa confirmed his ability to pick the right breaks on the right day, as the peloton let the break ride out to over an eight minute lead, and Costa bested other escapees such as Andreas Klöden (RadioShack Leopard) and Pierre Rolland (Europcar) by nearly a minute.

Fans won't see Costa attacking all day every day, but when he does, pay attention; because something exciting is guaranteed to happen.

ESCAPING, ON STAGE 16 OF THE 2013 TOUR

PUSHING HARD ON THE NEXT STAGE

ADAM
HANSEN

ADAM HANSEN (LOTTO SOUDAL) plays a dual role for his team; he is either a great breakaway rider, or a super-domestique. He will get food and drink for his team leaders. He will ride in the wind all day to keep them out of trouble. But give him the green light to race for himself, and he will be off in a flash.

Having finished a stage of the Giro d'Italia with a broken hand, and ridden 100km of a Tour de France stage with a broken collarbone, Hansen knows a good deal about pain. But he loves inflicting it on others just as much as enduring it himself.

'I give it 111 per cent. I just love to race,' he told *Cyclingtips* in 2013. 'But this is also a bad thing too. I'm smart enough to know that I should wait for final moves, but I love to mix it up and be where the action is when I should be sitting in, resting and waiting. It's not that I don't know better, [I] just love to race!'

It's fair to say Hansen sits on the same side of the fence as Jérémy Roy. It's all or nothing, and Hansen is all aggression.

Having spent a sizeable portion of his childhood in Hong Kong where he could go for months without ever actually going outside (thanks to a subway system integrated between his apartment building and his school), then progressing to a career as a computer programmer living back in Cairns, Australia, it does seem odd that his office is now the great outdoors.

But it's Hansen's attention to detail that parallels across all his careers. Some cyclists care very little for the equipment they receive, 'it's just a bike' and they just ride. Hansen, on the other hand, forges his own carbon shoes,

BREAKING AWAY ON STAGE 16 OF THE 2013 TOUR

continually adjusts his set-up and experiments with narrower bars or longer cranks.

And it's this inquisitive mind that can only be satiated by action. Given Hansen has ridden ten Grand Tours in a row (as of the 2014 Vuelta a España) it's understandable that sitting idle in the peloton is of no interest to him. So action for Hansen comes in the binary form: ride the front, or, attack!

Hansen's opportunism has seen him take stages from breakaways in both the Giro and the Vuelta, and he has come close multiple times at the Tour. In Rui Costa's previously

mentioned victorious Stage 16 of the 2013 Tour, Hansen was punching well above his weight on the final climb, launching an audacious attack that unhitched a number of climbing 'specialists'.

Hansen also joined Costa and Roy in another long breakaway in 2012 on Stage 18 from Blagnac to Brive-la-Gaillarde where the trio were part of a 16-man group attempting to outlast the sprinters' teams.

This was not, however, a simple chase and retrieve exercise for the peloton. At that stage in the Tour, there were 13 teams still without a stage win, thus every team without

LEANING INTO STAGE 14 OF THE 2012 TOUR

a sprinter were loading every break they could with their best riders. The end result: a break being driven by the likes of Hansen, Costa and Roy, with Alexandre Vinokourov (Astana), Patrick Gretsch (Argos-Shimano), David Millar (Garmin-Sharp), Edvald Boasson Hagen (Sky) and Michael Albasini (Orica-GreenEDGE) just to name a few, along for the ride.

The peloton and break fought a continual tug of war with the gap never going above four minutes, and with both collectives of riders splintering heavily towards the end of the race. In his element,

Hansen was one of the last survivors, launching a threatening solo move in the last 10km. It was, however, the strength of Mark Cavendish's then Team Sky lead-out train that trumped the Aussie's hopes for stage glory.

As a fan favourite, with a definite cult following, it's disappointing that Hansen is not let off the leash more often than he is, because excitement will always ensue. But do not lose faith, that elusive stage win is coming for the Aussie hardman, because breaking away is what he does best.

JENS
VOIGT

THERE COULD NEVER BE A BREAKAWAY SPECIALIST in world cycling more adored than Jens Voigt. Having finished every Tour de France between 2010 and his final Tour in 2014, Jens captured the hearts and minds of cycling fans worldwide. Known for his aggression laced with eccentricity, Jens has thrown out magnificent one-liners such as 'Shut up Legs,' and 'I'm motherfucking Jens Voigt' to the point that he has become an Arnold Schwarzenegger-like caricature in the cycling world. The fact that he chose to end his career with something as exceedingly painful as an attempt on the hour record (successful, but soon bested) also shows that like Hansen, Voigt has no aversion to pain.

Although stretching beyond recent years, Voigt's breakaway abilities have led him to two stage wins in the Tour, one in 2001 where he distanced Australian Brad McGee (Francaise des Jeux) after the duo left their five other escapees behind. And another in 2006 where Voigt was part of a five-man break given an astonishing 29 minute gap.

Voigt had told *Cyclingnews* in May of the 2005 that he wanted to move away from these long all day attacks, citing a low chance of victory as the main reason.

'Of course, it's great publicity to do long solos, it gives you a lot of sympathy from the public and great TV time for your sponsor,' Voigt said back in 2005. 'But an unspectacular victory is better than a spectacular death. So that's the new strategy: attack later to stand more chance of actually winning.'

Curiously he came out in 2006 and did the exact opposite of that, and he won a stage.

LEADING AN ESCAPE ON STAGE 14 OF THE 2011 TOUR

AND LEADING ON STAGE 1 OF THE 2014 TOUR

LEADING A CHASE ON STAGE 6 OF THE 2012 TOUR

In more recent times, on a short but hilly 125km Stage 20 from Annecy to Annecy-Semnoz in the 2013 Tour, Voigt proved his enthusiastic aggression by placing himself in the main break of the day. The 41-year-old, surrounded by riders almost half his size and almost half his age pushed a pace so ferocious that he left climbing specialists such as Rolland and Igor Anton (Euskaltel) in his wake. Although a fruitless pursuit in the end, given Team Sky with Chris Froome and Movistar with Nairo Quintana had scores to settle, Voigt took home the most aggressive as consolation.

Even more impressive for pure insanity was Voigt's attack on the opening stage of the 2014 Tour from Leeds to Harrogate. Having raced the Tour de France a staggering 17 times, Jens did not wait even a millisecond to enter the fray in his final foray. The very second the race director's flag dropped Jens bolted away from the pack, soon to be joined by Nicolas Edet (Cofidis) and Benoit Jarrier (Bretagne). Never let far out of sight of the peloton, Voigt went about crushing his companions taking the only King of the Mountain and Sprint points on offer and spending the last 50km of his escapade on his own. But being the opening stage and ending in a sprint, Mark Cavendish's Omega Pharma-Quick Step team and Marcel Kittel's Team Giant-Shimano were never going to let Voigt snatch the stage. A King of the Mountains jersey, a most aggressive dossard, and ongoing adoration did provide Voigt with some comfort.

There's little doubt that Jens Voigt finished his Tour de France career with more spectacular deaths than unspectacular victories, but that's exactly why his fans love him as they do. And that pervasive optimism is exactly why Trek Factory Racing are retaining Voigt's services as a coach, mentor and soon-to-be directeur sportif.

LEADING THE CHASE ON STAGE 12 OF THE 2011 TOUR

THOMAS
VOECKLER

THOMAS VOECKLER (EUROPCAR) is synonymous with the Tour de France. How else could one describe the home nation's hero who has spent 20 days in the yellow jersey—more than Fausto Coppi, Jan Ullrich or Vincenzo Nibali—won four stages, won the overall polka-dot jersey, finished third in the young rider category, finished every edition of the race since 2003, and finished as high up as fourth overall.

Voeckler is the ultimate example of a rider who has used his head to amass a palmarès far above what his physical capabilities suggest possible. But again, this is what makes cycling the world's most beautiful sport. It is not raced in a lab and the biggest lungs do not guarantee victory. In the rolling chess game that is the Tour de France, riders have to make crucial split-second decisions and few make them better than Voeckler.

In 2009, Voeckler (then Bouygues Telecom) took a gloriously cheeky victory having been part of an early break that 30km from the finish, sat just 40 seconds in front of the main bunch. The group ploughed on, however, and it was Voeckler who covered the right moves, and did just enough to counter-attack in the dying moments and hold off the peloton by seven seconds.

A year later Voeckler stamped a victory of a different kind when he simply rode away from his breakaway companions on the hilly 187.5km from Pamiers to Bagnères-de-Luchon. This day is better remembered in cycling annals for the 'Chaingate' scandal involving Andy Schleck and Alberto Contador, but for Voeckler, he took home a stage win that capped a tactically brilliant ride.

In 2012 Voeckler took yet another victory from a group of five during

the tenth stage, outwitting and outriding fellow breakaway specialist Jens Voigt. In Stage 16 of the same year Voeckler took a mountainous breakaway victory reminiscent of his 2010 success.

Simply put: Voeckler can win from a break on the flat or in the hills. His split-second decision making contributes greatly to this, but this ability is largely due another simple fact; he is cut-throat. He will not roll turns on the front of a break unless he has something to gain, and he will not hesitate to attack should a fortuitous opportunity present itself.

Stage 9 of the 2011 Tour de France was the fateful day that Johnny Hoogerland (Vacansoleil) and Juan Antonio Flecha (Sky) were side-swiped by a France Television media car and launched into a barbed wire fence. Immediately following the incident Voeckler put his head down and carried on. There was not even a moment of hesitation. He forced Luis Leon Sanchez (Rabobank) and Sandy Casar (Francaise des Jeux) to follow and continue the pace making.

The bottom line was that no rider was recovering from that crash quickly, and waiting would be a futile exercise. With a yellow jersey on the line it was always best to push on. Now there are deeper moral and ethical discussions to be had, but at the end of the day Thomas Voeckler is paid to win races, and by being absolutely ruthless, and swift in his decision making, Voeckler wins many. And nearly all of these victories come from breakaways.

ON STAGE 16 OF THE 2012 TOUR

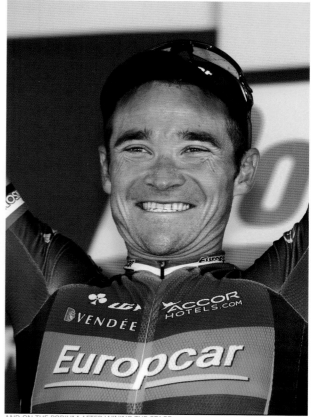

AND ON THE PODIUM AFTER WINING THE STAGE

VOECKLER (SECOND FROM RIGHT) WITH SAGAN, WIGGINS AND VAN GARDEREN ON THE PODIUM AFTER THE FINAL STAGE OF THE 2012 TOUR DE FRANCE

It's logical to assume that the winners of the previous five Tours de France were the five best general classification riders in those years. They were respectively, and in chronological order: Andy Schleck, Cadel Evans, Bradley Wiggins, Chris Froome and Vincenzo Nibali.

And you'd be right.

In any one of those years (and going back to the race's inception in 1903), among the race favourites there may have been a better climber, a better time triallist, a better *rouleur*, a better *puncheur*, a better tactician. But when you aggregate their proficiency across all disciplines and all areas, in each of these years, one of the aforementioned quintet came out on top and in front, and recorded the lowest overall time. And let's face it, *Le Tour* is all about time: saving seconds, gaining seconds (or in some cases, minutes), mitigating losses, augmenting advantages.

Interestingly, with Lance Armstrong's seven victories now rescinded, we haven't seen a back-to-back winner since Miguel Indurain, who won his fifth straight Tour in 1995, aged 31.

We no longer see one man dominate, and that's a good thing because the Tour is such a volatile and difficult beast, for one to slay it year after year with the aplomb of Armstrong (same goes for many of his predecessors) suggests quite clearly that something was wrong — very wrong. The US Anti-Doping Agency (USADA) dossier of October 2012 that brought down the Texan, among others, was the purging we had to have, and now that we've had it, professional cycling is all the better for it.

Can we be one-hundred per cent certain that what we've seen the past five Tours is for real?

One would like to think so, even if Schleck essentially won his Tour in court and Wiggins and Froome were scrutinised to the nth degree from the moment they donned the *maillot jaune* of race leader — many casting aspersions over the apparent ease of their victories, dubbing Team Sky 'UK Postal' (a none-too-subtle reference to Armstrong's US Postal Service team, via which he rode to 'victory' from 1999–2004).

What we can say is that cycling has arguably the most robust drug testing of any sport, Olympic or non-Olympic, and there are more tests done at the Tour than any other race on the calendar — or any other single sporting event, for that matter — by some margin. Perhaps more importantly, the culture of professional cycling is changing. Overwhelmingly, the thought of taking performance-enhancing substances is now anathema to the current generation of athletes, particularly the teens and twenty-somethings, and ultimately, it is this latter subset who will determine the future of this beautiful sport, for better (hopefully), or worse.

THE FIVE
GREAT GC RIDERS

ANDY SCHLECK   CADEL EVANS   BRADLEY WIGGINS   CHRIS FROOME   VINCENZO NIBALI

ANTHONY TAN

BEST OF 2010:
ANDY SCHLECK

HIS FATHER JONNY A FORMER professional and elder brother Frank, five years his senior, also plying his trade on two wheels, cycling was in Andy Schleck's blood.

Cyrille Guimard, the man who mentored then directed Bernard Hinault, Laurent Fignon, Lucien Van Impe and Greg LeMond to victory at the Tour, spotted a then 18-year-old Andy when he rode for the VC Roubaix cycling club in 2004, and said outright he was one of the greatest talents he had seen. From that point on, most assumed greatness—and victory in *La Grande Boucle*—would follow.

He appeared well on his way when, at 22 years, he won the young riders' classification and finished second overall to recidivist doper Danilo Di Luca at the 2007 Giro di Italia, before taking another white jersey one year and three months later—but this time at the biggest race of all (finishing 12th overall).

His 2009 Ardennes Classics campaign, where he finished second at La Flèche Wallonne and four days later emerged triumphant in Liège–Bastogne–Liège, gave rise to his most successful Tour outing to date; outdone only by a rampant Alberto Contador, whose greatest nemesis was not Schleck but his team-mate at the time ... Lance Armstrong.

Still, if he could finish runner-up at 25, when most professional cyclists enter their best years, he could win (perhaps even a few) within the next five to eight years, right?

With Contador just two and a half years his senior, Schleck the younger was up against arguably the best Grand Tour rider of his generation. Yet the

IN YELLOW AT THE END OF STAGE 9

AND STAGE 20

audacity of youth appeared to work in favour of Andy at the 2010 Tour. He inherited the *maillot jaune* from Cadel Evans after Stage 9, the third day in the Alps, and went into the final week—and the Pyrenees—with a 31-second advantage over the Spaniard nicknamed '*El Pistolero*'.

On the opening day of the Pyrenean troika, Schleck held his own, the pair finishing on the same time atop Ax 3 Domaines. But the next day, Stage 15 from Pamiers to Bagnères-de-Luchon, 2km from the summit of the *hors catégorie* climb of the Port de Balès and 23km from the finish, the Luxembourger launched a solo offensive, only to be struck by

mechanical mishap seconds later and forced to dismount to reengage a dropped chain.

Meanwhile, Contador countered and flew the coop with GC contenders Samuel Sánchez and Denis Menchov, among others, crossing the line 39 seconds in front of a fuming Schleck, who declared the day a showing of bad sportsmanship by a certain Spaniard from Pinto, who, despite jeers from the crowd, took over the race lead.

But was it? Opinion was divided about whether Contador should have waited or gone for it as he did; perhaps the sentiment was most aptly summed up by Ryder Hesjedal: 'If

you draw your sword and you drop it, you die.'

Ironically, after 3642km, Schleck lost the race by the same margin he trailed Contador by in Luchon. But in another fateful twist, and almost two years later, the former was declared the winner after the Court of Arbitration for Sport upheld Contador's positive test for clenbuterol, taken in Pau on the second rest day.

It proved to be the only Tour he would win before announcing his premature retirement in October 2014, aged 29.

SCHLECK AND CONTADOR ON STAGE 12 OF THE TOUR

LATER, ON STAGE 15

AHEAD ON STAGE 12

ATTACKING ON STAGE 15

BEST OF 2011:
CADEL EVANS

PRECOCIOUS FROM THE GET-GO, Cadel Evans was identified as a rare breed as early as 17 years old, when physiological tests at the Australian Institute of Sport showed he had the ability to absorb more oxygen than 99.9 per cent of the population, and was duly dubbed 'The Lung'.

At the time, few mountain bikers had made a successful transition from the dirt to road. But Tony Rominger, his manager at the time and a four-time Grand Tour winner, convinced him that the rewards that awaited this quirky character from Katherine could one day be immense ... and so it turned out.

Once under the tutelage of Aldo Sassi his rise was apparent, though given the doping zeitgeist, results were not immediate or remarkable. And despite his obvious predisposition towards multi-day tours he did not ride his first Tour de France till 2005, aged 28, riding for Belgian team Davitamon-Lotto, where he finished eighth to Armstrong, who has since had his victory (and six others) annulled. But from then on, for Evans, the rest, as they say, is history.

The Tour became an obsession—from eighth to fourth to second, to second again in 2008, the logical next step was the top step in Paris. But in 2009 the strength of Contador and the brothers Schleck, the return of Armstrong, and the emergence of Bradley Wiggins, coupled with less than happy times with his Flemish-speaking counterparts and sub-standard form, seemed at first to mark the beginning of the end of the road for Cadel.

Thankfully, as often in cycling (as in life), there was another twist in the tale.

Near the close of the 2009 season, the Road World Championships

WINNING STAGE 4

CHASING ON STAGE 18

HITTING THE STREETS OF PARIS ON STAGE 21

A EUPHORIC EVANS

in Mendrisio, Switzerland, marked a watershed moment: an uncharacteristic solo attack late in the race providing the never-say-die Aussie battler a launchpad to victory (an Australian first), keys to a new team, and a fully supported tilt at the Tour.

July 11 the following year and after the first mountain stage, the golden fleece was on his shoulders—though the celebration was short-lived. A crash the previous day later revealed a hairline fracture in his left elbow, which consequently saw him freefall in the standings 24 hours after inheriting the *maillot jaune*. He limped home to Paris almost an hour down, knowing that, by his own admission, he had 'two, maybe three' more chances left to win the prize that still eluded him.

By contrast and atypical for the incident-prone Evans, everything seemed to go right for Cadel in 2011 leading up to that year's *Grand Départ*. For once, it seemed, the stars had aligned in his favour.

His BMC Racing team caressed him through an accident-heavy opening week and a half, and while others like Wiggins and Contador came crashing down (and in the former's case, out), Evans and his coterie appeared to walk (or rather, ride) on water. A breakaway on Stage 9 that saw housewives' favourite Thomas Voeckler elevated into yellow for the next nine days proved the perfect scenario, as the assiduous Cadel bided his time till the penultimate day's time trial in Grenoble.

Andy Schleck rode a brilliant final week, capped off by victory on Stage 18 atop the Col du Galibier and the day after, the *maillot jaune*. But like so many times in his career, it was the race against the clock that proved the lanky Luxembourger's undoing; failing to recce the decisive 42.5km time test before the race began did nothing except place a final nail in the coffin.

The enormity of Evans' achievement made headlines around the world, including back home in Australia. Yet it wasn't till he returned to a hero's welcome in Melbourne's Federation Square that the man himself realised the extent of his doing and its effect on the Australian psyche.

Till his retirement in February 2015 at the eponymous Cadel Evans Great Ocean Road Race, he never again had it so good. But there will be only be one man from the land Down Under who first conquered the biggest bike race of all—and that, of course, is him.

BEST OF 2012:
BRADLEY WIGGINS

THE SECOND ANGLOPHONE in succession to win *Le Tour*, but unlike Evans' victory borne out of blood, sweat and tears, Bradley Wiggins' march from Liège to Paris was positively clinical.

Not since the doping heyday of Armstrong and co. have we seen such dominance by a man and his team; as a consequence the questions and innuendo came. So strong was Wiggins and Team Sky, 'the Kid from Kilburn', as he was dubbed, was never once worse than second on the *classement général*.

It's very likely that Wiggins, who unlike Armstrong has never failed a doping test and has long been vociferously anti-doping, rode 'paniagua' (derived from the Spanish term *pan y agua*, which translates to 'bread and water'). But his earlier friendship with Armstrong, combined with a lack of competition in that year's Tour (like the 2009 Tour where Astana teammates Armstrong and Contador fought between themselves, Wiggins' greatest threat came from within, in the form of teammate Christopher Froome) not to mention the ongoing investigation by the US Anti-Doping Agency, the contents of which surfaced three months after the 2012 Tour ended—raised the index of suspicion skywards, one might say.

Just as Evans' 2011 season was a blinder, equally, Wiggins' 2012 was an *annus mirabilis*.

Stage-race victories in Paris—Nice, the Tour de Romandie, then, auspiciously, three weeks before the *Grand Départ*, a second successive win at the Critérium du Dauphiné, it appeared this time round, he could do no wrong. All he need do was stay healthy and upright.

FLYING THE FLAG ON STAGE 20

Confirmation came when 'Wiggo' finished second to Fabian Cancellara in the 6.4km opener in Liège, seven seconds adrift of the Swiss powerhouse, who won a record fifth Tour prologue. But the first sign of dissension in the ranks came a week later in the Vosges mountain range when Froome left his leader behind to triumph at La Planche des Belles Filles. The upside was that Wiggins was now in yellow, but his teammate's impetuosity would prove a recurring theme throughout the rest of the Tour and beyond.

Wiggins demonstrated his resilience to those within and outside Team Sky by winning the first of two long individual time trials, extending his advantage over the defending champion by almost two minutes.

And while Cadel cracked in the Alps, Bradley showed bravura, his quintessential (albeit unexciting) tempo style enough to withstand Froome's frolicking on Stage 12 to La Toussuire, for which the latter copped a bollicking by management. Vincenzo Nibali, 27 at the time, was not yet at his peak despite having won the Vuelta a España two years prior; besides, his Liquigas-Cannondale team was no match for the metronomic Sky-bots, who rode up hill and down dale like clones programmed to destroy.

And so the final week became a procession. Hardly what the fans wanted, some who had camped by the roadside for days before, nor the hundreds of millions around the world, watching intently on TV,

waiting for the moment that defines a Tour and firmly places it into the annals of sporting history.

As virtuosic as the *maillot jaune* was in the final time trial, that moment never came.

Still, there was something quite exceptional about the way the boffins at Team Sky had reduced arguably the world's most romantic sport—at least the world's largest annual sporting event—into a game of numbers, and to their credit, come out on top. For them, *Le Tour* had become a scientific experiment: they had made the unpredictable, predictable, and rationalised the irrational.

Question was, could they do it again?

ON STAGE 11 OF THE SAME TOUR

SMILING ON STAGE 17

PUNCHING THROUGH ON STAGE 19

REACHING STAGE 20

BEST OF 2013:
CHRIS FROOME

IF BRADLEY WIGGINS IS THE quintessential larrikin Englishman, Christopher Froome is the polar opposite.

Brought up in Kenya rather than the backstreets of Kilburn; unfailingly polite as opposed to mercurial and occasionally foul-mouthed; and less a product of the British cycling system—or any other—than his own.

While the three Tour champions before him displayed a steady progression of results en route to becoming a Grand Tour contender-cum-winner, Froome's rise the past three seasons has been nothing short of meteoric. His breakthrough came at the 2011 Vuelta a España, when, as he would the following July, he was originally down to support Wiggins, but outshone his sometimes sideburned, sometimes bearded contemporary in the final week to finish second to another man from nowhere, Juan José Cobo of Spain.

Froome's trajectory from nobody to somebody was partly explained by bilharzia, a parasitic disease that he likely carried for much of his adult life. He was said to have suffered a recurrence in 2012, before making a full recovery prior to that year's Tour. When he and Wiggins went 1-2 in Paris, they became the first British riders to make the podium since the race's inception in 1903, and, despite a few moments of dissent, he was promised outright team leadership the following year. When Wiggins bombed out of the 2013 Giro d'Italia with a chest infection and dodgy knee, it became a fait accompli.

Conversely, and like Evans in 2011 and Wiggins the year previously, Froome's path to the *Grand Départ* in Corsica was seamless and confidence-boosting: overall victory at the Tour of Oman, followed by much of the same

LEAVING IT ALL BEHIND ON STAGE 11

ATTACKS ON STAGE 20

THE TEAM CELEBRATES ON STAGE 21

at the Critérium International, Tour de Romandie, and Critérium du Dauphiné.

A crash in the neutralised section of the first stage got his campaign off to a nervy start, but after that hiccup little troubled him. It appeared a near-carbon copy of the 2012 Tour handbook from Team Sky, when, like the previous year, Froome won the first mountain stage (this time to Ax 3 Domaines), but instead of Wiggins wearing yellow, it was he.

Prodigious as he was, 23-year-old Tour debutant Nairo Quintana and his Movistar homies were no match for the *maillot jaune* and his phalanx of men in black, while punchy 'Purito', a.k.a. Joaquim Rodríguez, paid for his lack of time-trial prowess, and Alberto Contador was off his A-game. For the remaining fortnight,

it became of question of not who would win, but by how much.

The exasperation was palpable.

For the second year running, the fans were treated to a 3500 kilometre Sky-led death march, their rival teams like prisoners of war, dragged around a lap of France by *domestiques* programmed to do nothing except drive their opposition into the ground. And for a second consecutive Tour, questions were been raised about Froome's faster-than-lightning succession to the throne, and whether this devastatingly effective yet incredibly boring *modus operandi* would be a sign of things to come for the next 10 years.

The centenary edition of the Tour was supposed to evoke memories and encourage superhuman feats of

years gone by, taking in classic climbs like Mont Ventoux and tackling the hairpin-heavy Alpe d'Huez twice in a day. Instead, we received another demonstration of death by numbers; the only sign of times of yore was the Stage 9 to Bagnères-de-Bigorre, when Team Sky was ambushed by Garmin-Sharp and Movistar, leaving Froome isolated for the first—and only—time in the race, as Irishman Daniel Martin prevailed on a day *Le Tour* was turned inside out and upside down.

Held for the first time at night, the finish on the Champs-Élysées was indeed spectacular—but everyone from Joe Average fan with his ham and cheese baguette, to VIPs sipping their martinis, to veteran cycling pundits, to riders and directeurs sportifs, were all thinking the same thing: how to derail the Sky Express?

AND AGAIN, FROOME IN FOCUS

BEST OF 2014:
VINCENZO NIBALI

ANSWER: LET THE SKY EXPRESS DERAIL THEMSELVES.

From the get-go, Froome appeared to be in similar shape to that of the previous year, finishing fifth on the first—a sprint stage, no less!—of a hat-trick of legs in the UK, won by Marcel Kittel, cycling's answer to Dolph Lundgren, who played Russian boxer Ivan Drago in *Rocky IV*.

Far more ominous was Vincenzo Nibali's derring-do twenty-four hours later. Fresh off his win at the Italian road championships a week prior, the 'Shark of Messina' smelled blood on the run-in to Sheffield, and with stage victory in hand, took a big bite out of his opponents' egos with the *maillot jaune* to boot.

However the bloodbath was yet to come.

The cobblestoned fifth stage saw more splits than a principal dancer from the Bolshoi Ballet, as fear of the stones and apocalyptic conditions combined to see the defending champ crash twice and leave the Tour in his team Jag, and all of Nibali's other main rivals lose a minimum two minutes.

Five days later, the Sicilian performed another hit-and-ride on the road to La Planche des Belles Filles, the scene of Froome's triumph two years previously, regaining the golden tunic he lost for a day. Alas, Nibali's only real rival, Alberto Contador, capitulated like Froome, crashing heavily, this time on a high-speed descent. According to some riders close by at the time, this was a consequence of unnecessarily risky manoeuvres. Whatever the real story, the Spaniard's quest for the throne would be delayed for another year, and in so doing, essentially provided a clear path to victory for Nibali—so long as he stayed upright and out of trouble.

Unfortunately for his rivals, it turned out to be a rather drawn-out death. Stage 13 to the Rhône-Alpes ski resort of Chamrousse—marking the first HC (*hors catégorie*—literally, out of category) climb of the Tour—precipitated the start of another feeding frenzy, and saw a third notch on the lapel for Nibali; the result of which put overnight second place Richie Porte out of contention, and simultaneously extending the lead to the man who replaced him, Alejandro Valverde, by more than three and a half minutes.

The following day to Risoul in the Hautes-Alpes, the Italian switched to auto-pilot—yet nevertheless extended his advantage to the aging Valverde, at 34 years nearly five years his senior, by one minute more. Meanwhile, Frenchmen Romain Bardet and Thibaut Pinot, third and fourth respectively and riding creditably, nonetheless found themselves languishing, both around five minutes behind ... and still with a week remaining.

Victory was assured but Nibali showed no mercy, the troika of Pyrenean legs doing nothing except to widen an already cavernous—not to mention embarrassing—lead. On the third day to Hautacam, the Italian brutally toyed then dispensed those nearest to him on the overall classification, which by any measure wasn't very near at all. Seven minutes—*seven!*—clear of his closest three competitors, and while most wished for the humiliation to end there and then (perhaps including Nibali himself), there still remained a 54km race against the clock; for posterity's sake, a double-digit advantage by Paris was a scenario no-one wanted to see.

Naturally, with his chasm-sized lead, Nibali wasn't taking any risks, yet at the same time wanted to honour the *maillot jaune*. Outside of the specialists including stage winner Tony Martin and Tom Domoulin and Jan Bárta, second and third respectively, he ended up best of the rest—and was also the only GC contender to arrive in Périgueux within two minutes of the three-time world time-trial champion.

Far more intriguing, however, was the battle for second and third in Paris. Valverde was tipped to move from fourth to second but stayed where he was, while Jean-Christophe Péraud, all of 37 years young, showed how to grow old gracefully; a superlative ride by the Beijing Games cross country mountain-bike silver medallist elevating the Frenchman from third to second, while his compatriot Thibaut Pinot, with legs 13 years fresher but not yet as strong, came of age to secure a place on the final podium.

Despite enjoying the largest winning margin of the last 17 years—three minutes more than first to second in 2013, and four minutes more than 2012—Nibali was given only a light dusting from the wizened journalists in the Tour de France *salle de presse*, where umpteen reams of words are bashed out on portable computers each day and flung far and wide across the globe.

Is he more credible than Wiggins or Froome? His career has certainly been one of steady progression; by contrast the others' rise has been less so. Is he more likeable than Wiggins or Froome? Inside the UK, no; outside, unequivocally.

Whatever the case, Nibali was the best of 2014, in a way that can only be described as a lay down misere.

PART OF THE PACK ON STAGE 19

NIBALI AND KONIG IN ACTION ON STAGE 13

ALONE ON STAGE 20

ON THE PODIUM

Ask anyone to name their favourite all-time stage in the Tour de France and nine times out of ten the response will involve ample climbs and punishment. Sprints are a sensational, albeit short-lived, spectacle, but there's something truly compelling about watching spindly men do battle up a steep slope in slow motion. Some of the best duels of the sport have had mountains as their backdrop. When us amateurs dream of riding a stage of the Tour, it is not a flat schlep across the Loire valley, but the fabled cols of Ventoux, Alpe d'Huez, Galibier and the Tourmalet that get the juices flowing.

Climbing marvels such as Fausto Coppi, Federico Bahamontes, Charly Gaul and Lucien Van Impe paved the way for an explosive Nineties in which the likes of Marco Pantani, Claudio Chiappucci, Pedro Delgado and Richard Virenque all added to the Pyrenean and Alpine myth. This was an era when the climbing benchmark was measured by the Tour's famous polka dot jersey, as lean, wiry, whippet-like mountain goats danced their lithe, almost skeletal figures to a succession of summits. Add to the mix the bulkier powerhouses in the mould of Jan Ullrich or Miguel Indurain who, with slow-beating hearts and lungs like balloons, combined brute force and a diesel engine to adapt their time-trialling skills to high gradients.

There's no denying that climbing lost some of its magic during Lance Armstrong's reign. As the *maillot à pois* lost its relevance, riders started to play the game to pick up points—hence former French sprinter Laurent Jalabert's two polka dot jerseys (2001/02) and those of compatriots Anthony Charteau (2010) and Thomas Voeckler (2012). The tempo riding and high-wattage monotony of Team Sky's endless computation of power and weight deprived the Tour of the kind of panache that got so many of us hooked in the first place.

Nutrition plans, marginal gains and metronomic pedalling reduced the sport to a science. But the tide is turning. Back-to-back robotic Team Sky wins gave way to the victory of an uphill aesthete in Vincenzo Nibali in 2014, while a new breed of climbing Colombians led by Nairo Quintana is on the rise. Double mountain stage winner Rafal Majka is the purest of climbers, while rising Irish star Dan Martin doesn't even use a power meter. For the Tour's climbing fans, things are on the rise.

FIVE OF THE BEST
TOUR DE FRANCE CLIMBERS

ALEJANDRO
VALVERDE

PIERRE
ROLLAND

SAMUEL
SÁNCHEZ

CHRISTOPHE
RIBLON

JURGEN
VAN DEN BROECK

FELIX LOWE

ALEJANDRO
VALVERDE

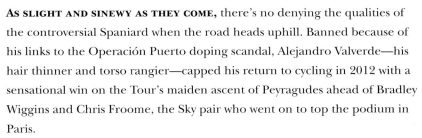

AS SLIGHT AND SINEWY AS THEY COME, there's no denying the qualities of the controversial Spaniard when the road heads uphill. Banned because of his links to the Operación Puerto doping scandal, Alejandro Valverde—his hair thinner and torso rangier—capped his return to cycling in 2012 with a sensational win on the Tour's maiden ascent of Peyragudes ahead of Bradley Wiggins and Chris Froome, the Sky pair who went on to top the podium in Paris.

Bonking with gusto in the Alps a week earlier en route to La Toussuire—despite being in the initial main break—Valverde was part of the day's early escape in Stage 17 before riding clear on the Port de Balès climb 35km from the finish. His lead dropped to little over a minute at the start of the fifth and final climb to Peyragudes, but 'El Imbatido' (The Unbeaten) used his experience to defy the chasing Sky duo to take a fourth career Tour win in the Pyrenean ski resort.

A year later Valverde showed that, individually, he still had what it takes to put up a fight against Sky's overpowering collective entity. In the first major mountain showdown of the 2013 Tour, Valverde placed third at Ax 3 Domaines behind Froome and Richie Porte—taking time off team-mate Nairo Quintana and fellow Spaniard Alberto Contador in the process. An unlucky mechanical in Stage 13 saw him lose the best part of 10 minutes in the crosswinds en route to Saint-Amand-Monrond but a typically strong showing in the Alps saw him salvage eighth place in the general classification.

Expectations were high for the Spanish veteran entering the 2014 Tour. In the absence of Giro d'Italia-winning Quintana, Valverde was Movistar's main man—and a third place behind French tyro Thibaut Pinot and Italy's Vincenzo Nibali, wearing the yellow jersey, at La Planche des Belles Filles was followed by fourth at Chamrousse three days later. Lacking the explosivity of his earlier years, Valverde was consistent in the Alps and Pyrenees, finishing tenth at Risoul, Saint Lary and Hautacam before taking fourth overall in Paris—his best ever finish in the Tour.

There's no denying that Valverde's strongest years are behind him—but his topping the UCI WorldTour rankings for a third time in 2014 underlines his remarkable longevity. Wiry and wily, Valverde has certainly become a more cautious rider as he matures—something perhaps related to the likely shift in his training methods since the two-year ban that struck him down in his prime.

As a climber, Valverde's main strength comes in his ability to put in short and sharp accelerations to distance his rivals. Matched in these trademark uphill bursts perhaps only by compatriot Joaquim Rodríguez, his knack of seemingly sprinting up punchy climbs is no better exemplified than in his fine record in the Ardennes classics and other lumpy one-day races over the years. His critics, however, will flag up his lack of remorse and the spineless nature in which he never confessed to blood doping, merely accepting, begrudgingly, the back-dated sanction that followed the seizure of blood bags containing his DNA and labelled with the name of his dog, Piti.

This is a pity, for despite his unrepentant streak there remains something honest and pared down about Valverde's climbing prowess. That he was further cast as the pantomime villain in the 2014 Tour—this time as the Punch to Pinot's Judy, after an uncharacteristically rare incident of sandbagging—merely underlines his canny adaptability as his powers inevitably diminish. There's a certain swagger with Valverde that's hard not to admire; to this day he is still one of cycling's great entertainers—almost wholly down to his capacity for dancing uphill with the elegance of a bullfighting ballerina.

The full range of Valverde's climbing armoury has admittedly been more apparent in the Vuelta—where he's recorded eight stage wins and one overall title. But it is his timeless faculty of climbing with the very best that has seen Valverde only ever finish once outside the top eight in thirteen completed Grand Tours. 2014 may have seen him ultimately pipped to the podium by Pinot and Jean-Christophe Péraud, but his consistent and mostly aggressive climbing since 2010 in the world's biggest bike race puts 'The Green Bullet' ahead of the French duo in a current hall of fame.

Valverde claims that 2014 was his best season yet. Despite Quintana returning to the fold in 2015, the Spaniard is still hungry for a Tour podium. Whether the Colombian's presence will free the Spaniard up for a pop at the polka dot jersey remains to be seen. Were Valverde to capture the race's mountains jersey it would be a worthy addition to what is arguably one of the most impressive palmarès in modern cycling.

LEADING AN ESCAPE ON STAGE 11 OF THE 2012 TOUR

PINOT AND VALVERDE ON STAGE 8 OF THE 2014 TOUR

STAGE 17 OF THE 2014 TOUR

PIERRE
ROLLAND

● ● ● ● ● ● ● ● ● ● ● ● ● ● ● ● ● ●

IT IS PERHAPS A TRIFLE IRONIC to include in a list of the Tour's top climbers a man whose hapless (and ultimately entirely fruitless) quest for the polka dot jersey in 2013 made him a figure of ridicule among fans and riders alike. But more on that later.

Before Messieurs Pinot and Bardet burst onto the scene, Pierre Rolland was the next great hope for French cycling. Deprived of an overall winner since Bernard Hinault and of an out-and-out climber since Richard Virenque, here was a raw talent capable of perhaps delivering on both counts. Given his recent ubiquity in the peloton it's easy to overestimate Rolland's age: although a relative veteran of six Tours, the softly spoken Frenchman is still only 28 years old, despite possessing the same pale, almost cherubic, choir boy features of the rider who finished twentieth in his debut Tour in 2009, less than three months before his 22nd birthday.

Besides a newly-found penchant for nasal strips, little has changed with 'Pierrot'. Although now a marked man, Rolland is one of the few riders in the peloton who takes regular, considerable risks by attacking from distance. Without a team of equally strong climbing domestiques to deliver him, Team Sky-style, to the foot of the final climb, Rolland often takes things into his own hands. More often than not, he does so with brio. Capable of holding his own with the top favourites, Rolland seems equally at ease when riding alone and defying the odds. Canny and calculating, he also boasts an admirably languid pedal stroke—a distinct climbing style that is arguably the most aesthetically pleasing of all his peers.

WINNING STAGE 19 OF THE 2011 TOUR

ESCAPING WITH HESJEDAL ON STAGE 9 OF THE 2013 TOUR

Rolland came of age in 2011 when expertly shepherding team leader Thomas Voeckler through two mountain ranges during the popular Frenchman's famous second ten-day stint in yellow, which resulted in unexpected top ten finishes for the Europcar pair at Luz Ardiden, Plateau de Beille and on the mighty Galibier. So impressive was Rolland in the role of Voeckler's domestique de luxe that a watching Lance Armstrong referred to him as a 'rockstar' on Twitter. But the best was to come.

When Tommy cracked on the race's second visit to the Galibier in Stage 19, Rolland got the green light to pursue his own ambitions. He chased down Alberto Contador and Andy Schleck to reach the foot of Alpe d'Huez in the lead alongside Ryder Hesjedal. Double Tour winner Contador caught and passed the leaders, but Rolland was only just getting into his stride. Having trained on the mythical climb all spring, he later admitted with exquisite nonchalance that on the first of twenty-one hairpins he could simply 'put it in the big ring and ride à bloc to the finish'.

It was not merely his strength that delivered him to the line, but timing and guile: using Samuel Sánchez as a foil, Rolland returned to the wheel of Contador before launching his killer blow on the last hairpin with 2km remaining. Eurosport's French commentators basked in this 'one-man show formidable' as Rolland rode into the white jersey and delivered a belated first home stage win of the race. He was the first Frenchman to win atop the Alpe since Hinault in 1986—the year Rolland was born.

One year after finishing eighth in Paris, Rolland's GC hopes took an even larger pasting than usual before the mountains. A combination of crosswinds and his lingering inability to ride against the clock meant Rolland was already ten minutes down before rising from the dead in the Alps. Eighth on the day Voeckler won in Bellegarde-sur-Valserine, Rolland soloed to his own victory at La Toussuire one day later. (If the win didn't make the headlines that it perhaps deserved, this was largely down to the intriguing incident that saw Chris Froome ride clear of Sky team-mate Bradley Wiggins, the yellow jersey, on the final ascent before receiving strict team orders to slow down.)

But what of his doomed and lampooned assault on the polka dot jersey in 2013? After all, such a prize would seem fitting for such an accomplished climber. That may be, but the way Rolland went about his pursuit of polka dots, after he dropped out of GC contention following the first of two long time trials, earned him much derision. Overexcited, Rolland committed the fashion faux pas of combining his jersey not only with spotted shorts, gloves, socks and helmet, but a customised paint job on his Colnago. A whopping forty-three minutes down after the second individual time trial, the former conqueror of lofty peaks was reduced to picking up points here and there over minor summits before eventually losing out to both Froome and Nairo Quintana in the Alps.

With Europcar gaining WorldTour status next season, Rolland freshened his race programme up to include a maiden stab at the Giro, where he finished fourth despite the kind of early setbacks that you would expect from Europcar and the team time-trial discipline. His exertions meant Rolland had to lower his expectations in the Tour, his best result coming with a sixth at Pla d'Adet. Although he only narrowly missed out on the top ten, Rolland was overshadowed by countryman Jean-Christophe Péraud and Thibaut Pinot (who both made the podium) and sixth-place Romain Bardet.

No longer worn down by the mantle of being France's next big thing, perhaps the worldly-wise Pierrot can now take things up a level. The route of the 2015 Tour is climber-friendly and features just fourteen individual time trial kilometres. Rolland must be licking his lips in anticipation.

WINNING STAGE 19 OF THE 2011 TOUR

SAMUEL
SÁNCHEZ

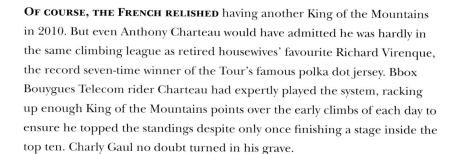

OF COURSE, THE FRENCH RELISHED having another King of the Mountains in 2010. But even Anthony Charteau would have admitted he was hardly in the same climbing league as retired housewives' favourite Richard Virenque, the record seven-time winner of the Tour's famous polka dot jersey. Bbox Bouygues Telecom rider Charteau had expertly played the system, racking up enough King of the Mountains points over the early climbs of each day to ensure he topped the standings despite only once finishing a stage inside the top ten. Charly Gaul no doubt turned in his grave.

In an attempt to see a bona fide climber seize back the polka dots, Tour organisers ASO changed the points system ahead of the 2011 race—and their decision was vindicated from the get-go thanks to the consistent uphill animation of Spaniard Samuel Sánchez. Before Euskaltel-Euskadi relaxed their regional recruitment policy to open their frontiers to foreigners in a bid to keep the team alive, all-rounder Sánchez was one of a very few riders not born in the Basque Country to wear the team's eye-catching orange kit. Born in Oviedo in Asturias, Sánchez had raced in the region as an amateur and so became a joyfully adopted son.

Sánchez is often viewed as the kind of climber who will throw caution to the wind, attack at any moment and shrug off both circumstance and odds. He was certainly one of a select few capable of animating a race by refusing to kowtow to the kind of numbed tempo-fuelled hegemony that Team Sky once inflicted upon the peloton. If rival Denis Menchov was 'The Silent Assassin' then Sánchez was about as subtle as James Bond in a quaint Tuscan hilltop town.

WINNIG STAGE 12 OF THE 2011 TOUR

That's not to say that Sánchez, for all his aggressive live-wire qualities, could not be tactically astute. Take his first ever Tour stage win, for instance. One of the few pure climbers whose descending skills were a match for his uphill prowess, Sánchez took advantage of the GC men marking themselves in the notoriously attritional 2011 Tour and slipped away as the main pack approached the Col du Tourmalet during Stage 12. Taking Belgian revelation Jelle Vanendert with him, the 2008 Olympic road-race champion joined forces with team-mate Rubén Plaza—who was part of the earlier break—before he and Vanendert reeled in the lingering escapees on the *hors catégorie* Luz-Ardiden summit finish. With the thought of his narrow loss in Morzine a year previously no doubt fresh in his mind, Sánchez used his experience to shell his rival on the final straight to take an emphatic victory—to the rapture of the numerous Basque supporters who had crossed the Spanish border to see their hero in action.

Two days later, Vanendert would get his own back with victory on Plateau de Beille ahead of second-place Sánchez, despite the Spaniard's late surge on the tortuous Pyrenean climb. If Sánchez was slightly off the boil a week later on the Galibier, it was perhaps because he was keeping his powder dry for the next day's final mountain showdown on Alpe d'Huez. Pierre Rolland denied him a second win of the race on the legendary col, but another second place secured Sánchez the polka dot jersey, the first Spaniard to do so in 37 years.

It should be added that Sánchez had already proved his climbing mettle on the Grande Boucle before his star performance in 2011. A year earlier, he had been agonisingly pipped to a maiden mountain win by Andy Schleck in Morzine-Avoriaz before finishing second, again, at Ax 3 Domaines and fourth on the Tourmalet. With both Alberto Contador and Menchov eventually rubbed out of the record books, Sánchez would later, retrospectively, be made runner-up behind Schleck

in the final standings.

Returning to the Tour in 2012 to defend his King of the mountains title, Sánchez was in stellar form after a mountain-top win set up his overall triumph in the Tour of the Basque Country. But a nasty crash in Stage 7 forced him out, effectively reducing Euskaltel to a fry-up without the bacon. The after-effects of the crash lingered long into next season, where Sánchez focused on the Giro and not the Tour. After an eleventh-hour switch to BMC in 2014 following the demise of Euskaltel, Sánchez once again skipped the Tour in a bid to support Cadel Evans in the Giro and lead the team in the Vuelta, where he placed sixth. Following a period of uncertainty, Sánchez finally signed a year-long extension with BMC in January 2015. A return to the race which he so animated in 2010 and 2011 is unlikely, with the Spaniard assuming more of a supportive role for BMC's emerging talents. The Tour will be all the poorer without the uphill *pédaleur de charme* they call 'Samu'.

CONTADOR, MENCHOV AND SANCHEZ DESCENDING ON STAGE 15 OF THE 2010 TOUR

CAVENDISH, GOSS, SAGAN AND SANCHEZ AT THE END OF STAGE 18 OF THE 2012 TOUR

CHRISTOPHE
RIBLON

● ● ● ● ● ● ● ● ● ● ● ● ● ● ● ● ● ● ●

NOW TO A VERY DIFFERENT TYPE OF CLIMBER: a track specialist who rarely excels when the gradient creeps towards double digits, but one who has incongruously targeted the mountains as a favoured playground. Step forward Frenchman Christophe Riblon, an AG2R-La Mondiale mainstay who has notched two high mountain stage wins in the past five years—including the Tour's first ever double ascent of Alpe d'Huez. And to think, things could have been so different had a disillusioned Riblon been allowed to quit the 2010 Tour on the eve of the Pyrenees ...

After finishing seventh in the Dauphiné in June, Riblon entered that Tour with hopes of making an impression in the GC—despite still juggling his road and track aspirations. Not reaching the heights he had anticipated in the opening fortnight of the race, Riblon had to be talked out of throwing in the towel by his team manager at the finish of stage 13 in Revel. The 29-year-old didn't take long to turn things round: the next day he was part of an eight-man break as the race entered the mountains. Breaking clear on the penultimate climb, Riblon crested the summit of the Port de Pailhères before soloing to a magnificent win at Ax 3 Domaines—his first on the Tour—as the protracted poker battle between favourites Alberto Contador and Andy Schleck played out in his wake.

'The track is very important in my career,' Riblon said afterwards. 'I've shown that it is possible to do the track and be a good climber. I don't consider myself a great climber like Contador, but I'm a good one. I used to watch climbers like Marco Pantani and Thierry Claveyrolat when I was young

and it's been my dream since I started cycling as a six-year-old to do good things at the Tour and more than twenty years later my dreams have come true.' His best was yet to come—but it would take patience. For Riblon's best results next year in the mountains came with a solid if unspectacular twentieth place atop Plateau de Beille. And while Pierre Rolland was securing France's only stage win in 2011 on Alpe d'Huez, Riblon was pedalling squares to cross the line almost thirteen minutes down on his compatriot. Little did anyone know—not least the unsuspecting French public—that Riblon would use the race's next visit

to Alpe d'Huez to write his own piece of history.

Another barren year followed in 2012 with Riblon's best mountain placing being a humdrum twenty-seventh in Peyragudes as Alejandro Valverde marked his comeback with a solo win. When Riblon toiled to fifty-fifth on Mont Ventoux one year later, things looked ominous for his prospects in the one-hundredth Tour. But a day later, he found himself in the main break and missed out on the stage win in Gap only after Rui Costa attacked in a monsoon on the Col du Manse. Two days later, Riblon wouldn't settle for second-best again.

As part of the Tour's centenary celebrations ASO had decided to send the riders up Alpe d'Huez twice in one afternoon—either side of an unprecedented detour up the barren Col du Sarenne. Riblon was part of a three-man break alongside Tejay Van Garderen and Moreno Moser that completed the first ascent of the twenty-one hairpins with a healthy gap over the main pack. Double disaster struck on the perilous descent of the Sarenne as Van Garderen dropped a chain and Riblon rode wide into a ditch. But both men recovered to drop Moser on the final climb.

Van Garderen looked to have the

LEADING AN ESCAPE ON STAGE 7 OF THE 2009 TOUR

PUSHING IT ON STAGE 10 OF THE 2014 TOUR

win in the bag but Riblon fought back to catch and pass the American with just 2km remaining—at exactly the same spot where Rolland put in his own decisive attack two years previously. Riblon's emphatic win in the Centenary Tour's queen stage came three years to the day after his maiden victory at Ax 3 Domaines. Like Rolland's, it was France's first and only win that year, securing Riblon his nation's prestigious Vélo d'Or award.

In a bid to emulate the 2013 Tour riders, I rode a double ascent of Alpe d'Huez myself two months later. I notched off those tortuous 42 hairpins one by one, dodged the roaming sheep and potholes on the Sarenne, and even stopped to dip my toe in the same ditch where Riblon came a cropper. I have nothing but admiration for his achievement that day: it was one of the best performances by a Frenchman in recent memory. One year later it was followed by the best Tour for the home nation in a quarter of a century, with two Frenchmen—Jean-Christophe Péraud and Thibaut Pinot—finishing on the podium below Vincenzo Nibali.

With his climbing team-mates Peraud and Romain Bardet (who finished sixth) carrying the torch for France, Riblon's own role in his seventh consecutive Tour was very much reduced to that of a domestique. So much is expected of both Peraud and Bardet in 2015 that it would be a surprise were Riblon, 34, to add to his unlikely collection of mountain scalps. But his name will always adorn one corner of Alpe d'Huez—and besides Rolland, the great Bernard Hinault is the only other Frenchman who can currently make such a boast. Illustrious company for a chancer from the track.

WINNING STAGE 13 OF THE 2010 TOUR

JURGEN
VAN DEN BROECK

● ● ● ● ● ● ● ● ● ● ● ● ● ● ● ● ● ●

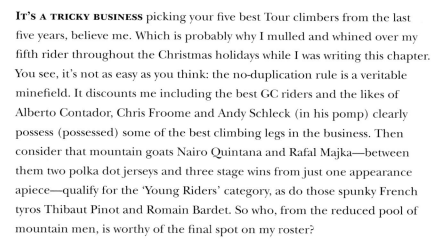

IT'S A TRICKY BUSINESS picking your five best Tour climbers from the last five years, believe me. Which is probably why I mulled and whined over my fifth rider throughout the Christmas holidays while I was writing this chapter. You see, it's not as easy as you think: the no-duplication rule is a veritable minefield. It discounts me including the best GC riders and the likes of Alberto Contador, Chris Froome and Andy Schleck (in his pomp) clearly possess (possessed) some of the best climbing legs in the business. Then consider that mountain goats Nairo Quintana and Rafal Majka—between them two polka dot jerseys and three stage wins from just one appearance apiece—qualify for the 'Young Riders' category, as do those spunky French tyros Thibaut Pinot and Romain Bardet. So who, from the reduced pool of mountain men, is worthy of the final spot on my roster?

How about Jurgen van den Broeck? The rangy Belgian is one of those cyclists who is rarely visible throughout the year but always crops up at the Tour touted as a podium possible. To be fair, he's rarely visible on the Tour either—which, conversely, is a compliment of sorts. Riders like VDB rely on stealth, grit, determination and consistency. His predecessor at Lotto—a certain Cadel Evans—was similar in many respects bar one: the Australian actually won races by the bucket load, including the 2011 Tour. One mountain scalp from the 2011 Dauphiné aside, VDB is as winless as they come.

Over the years, van den Broeck has nevertheless cemented his status as Belgium's best grimpeur. This, in turn, has made the 32-year-old fairly reliable: if he doesn't crash out of a major race (like he did in the 2011 or 2013 Tours) then he'll finish in the top 15. Taller and heavier than most climbers, van den Broeck is about as explosive as Guy Fawkes's failed Gunpowder Plot. Instead, he relies on a purring diesel engine much in the same way as Ivan Basso or, before him, Jan Ullrich. This powerful engine saw VDB crowned a junior world time-trial champion before a switch in focus to climbing in his late 20s meant his individual time trial technique suffered accordingly.

Lacking the explosiveness of a Quintana or an uphill sprint kick à la Valverde, van den Broeck is yet to win a Tour stage since his debut in 2009, his best finish being third place at Mende in 2010. This was the year that van den Broeck became Lotto's GC man following Evans's switch to BMC, the Australian having grown frustrated with sharing team leadership with another Belgian, Philippe Gilbert. Van den Broeck would suffer a similar plight, his

GC ambitions on the Belgian team always playing second fiddle to André Greipel's sprint train. He nevertheless rode to fifth place on the Tour—rising to third following the retrospective disqualification of winner Contador and third-place Denis Menchov.

A year later, VDB withdrew after crashing heavily in the nasty downhill pile-up on the Col du Pas de Peyrol that saw Alexandre Vinokourov break his femur in Stage 9. In his absence (VDB fractured his shoulder blade and ribs, plus punctured a lung) his solitary climbing domestique, Jelle Vanendert, came out of his shell to win atop Plateau de Beille amid a string of strong mountain performances. It was on the climb to La Planche des Belles Filles one year later where van den Broeck's GC hopes ended—but he recovered in the Alps to rise to a fourth-place finish in the Centenary Tour. His status as a bit-part player,

however, was underlined in the stage to Peyragudes when van den Broeck was caught in the crossfire as Froome pulled clear from his Sky team-mate, Bradley Wiggins, in yellow. It seemed like he had gatecrashed some kind of domestic altercation.

Another fall ended VDB's chances in 2013 while he failed to take advantage of the dual withdrawals of Contador and Froome in 2014, finishing thirteenth in Paris after an indifferent three weeks in France. But with team-mate Vanendert unable to repeat his heroics of 2011, van den Broeck remains the most consistent climber in Belgian cycling—although he claims his love/hate relationship with the Tour will be put on ice in 2015 while he sets his sights on a Giro-Vuelta double. 'The Tour podium is still a dream', he claimed in late 2014. You get the sense that a mountain stage victory would be a better target— and, if it happens, entirely deserved.

ON THE 2010 TOUR

LEADING ON STAGE 4 OF THE 2011 TOUR

IN ACTION ON STAGE 13 OF THE 2014 TOUR

THE TOUR DE FRANCE IS A TEAM EVENT LIKE NO OTHER. THERE IS ONLY ONE *maillot jaune*, BUT THAT ONE JERSEY CANNOT BE WON WITHOUT THE SUPPORT OF A STRONG AND LOYAL TEAM. A TEAM MEANS EACH LEADER HAS AN ARMY OF TEAMMATES, SOIGNEURS (CARERS OR 'HELPERS'), PHYSIOTHERAPISTS, MASSEURS, MECHANICS, MANAGERS, TECHNICAL STAFF *and* A LOT OF EXPENSIVE EQUIPMENT ALL COMPILED WITH THE COMMON GOAL OF ENSURING SAID LEADER CROSSES A LINE QUICKER THAN HIS OPPONENTS. THE TOUR DE FRANCE IS NEVER JUST CHRIS FROOME VERSUS NAIRO QUINTANA; IT'S SKY VERSUS MOVISTAR. IT IS MARK CAVENDISH'S ETIXX-QUICK STEP (FORMERLY OMEGA PHARMA-QUICK STEP) SPRINT TRAIN VERSUS MARCEL KITTEL AND TEAM GIANT-ALPECIN (FORMERLY GIANT-SHIMANO). THE GREATEST BATTLES AND DRAMAS OVER THE YEARS OF THE TOUR DE FRANCE HAVE BEEN BORN FROM A TEAM NARRATIVE.

IN RECENT HISTORY, THE BIRTH OF BOTH SKY AND ORICA-GREENEDGE, THE SUCCESSES AND QUESTION MARKS OVER ASTANA, THE INFLUENCE OF BJARNE RIIS, OLEG TINKOV AND THEIR TINKOFF-SAXO TEAM AS WELL AS THE RACE DEFINING ATTACKS BY MOVISTAR HAVE KEPT FANS INTRIGUED. THE TWO-WHEELED THEATRE OF THE TOUR DE FRANCE IS EVER-UNFOLDING, AND HERE ARE THE TOP FIVE TEAM TALES.

TOP TEAM TALES
FROM LE TOUR

SKY   ORICA-GREENEDGE   MOVISTAR   TINKOFF-SAXO   ASTANA

JONATHAN LOVELOCK

TEAM SKY:
DIVIDE AND CONQUER

NO TEAM HAS MADE MORE HEADLINES in the Tour de France in recent years than Team Sky. Sky has won two Tours, it has changed the way the race is ridden, and it has provided the ultimate tabloid fodder with the ongoing Chris Froome–Bradley Wiggins feud.

In February 2009 Team Sky was announced with a vision of having a British born winner of Tour de France within five years. BSkyB's relationship with British Cycling started with a modest investment of £1m in the form of the Sky Track Cycling team. Soon after Sir Dave Brailsford, now Team Sky Principal, convinced BSkyB Chairman James Murdoch to commit to a pro road cycling team. And with investments of £14,603m and £16,680m in 2010 and 2011 alone, commit Murdoch did.

It's fair to say, however, after Sky's first Tour de France efforts in 2010, the cycling world was dismissive of the new kids on the block. Bradley Wiggins finished a disappointing 24th and the team had very little to write home about. In 2011 things looked to be turning up with Wiggins coming into the Tour a strong contender having won the Tour of California, the Critérium du Dauphiné and finished 3rd at Paris–Nice. As is often the case, however, the nerves of the first week, cross winds and narrow roads left Wiggins at the bottom of a pile-up late in Stage 7. The Sky leader could do little other than cradle a cracked collarbone on the side of the road as he watched the peloton ride away.

2012 is where Team Sky took over the headlines for all of the right, and wrong, reasons. Late in 2011 at the Vuelta a España, Chris Froome was still considered second in command and made to ride in support of Wiggins. Although it was soon evident that Froome was the superior climber, he was made to wait and pace Wiggins, ultimately sacrificing his own chances of victory. When it became clear Wiggins' ship was sunk, Froome was given the green light to race for himself, but he was not able to recoup the time he had already conceded to eventual winner Juan José Cobo (Geox-TMC). Any root-cause analysis on Team Sky's leadership feuds would find first fault in the personality differences between Wiggins and Froome, but the 2012 Vuelta would prove catalytic in kick-starting the process.

At the 2012 Tour de France, Wiggins was the dedicated team leader. And Team Sky strangled the race with their dominating mono-paced tempo. With Kanstantsin Siutsou, Christian Knees, Michael Rogers, Richie Porte and Froome all ready to drive the pace on the climbs before Wiggins even hit the wind, nothing except a crash would stop the Sky train. But the real drama would come on Stages 11 and 17 where Froome drove the pace such that he left his leader behind, and had to be radioed and told to slow down. Some questionable gestures from Froome to Wiggins for the

world to see on Stage 17 did nothing to calm what appeared to be a rapidly widening rift.

In his memoir *The Climb*, released in 2014, Froome gave a glimpse into the disquiet, stating that the team 'rode around him [Wiggins] and his moods like he was a traffic island'. Froome also claimed that Wiggins withheld Froome's post tour bonus, which is a serious faux pas in the cycling word. It is tradition for the Tour winner to pay his teammates and team staff a hefty bonus from the circa 450,000 winners cheque.

No doubt the media ate up the drama at the time, but regardless of internal troubles, Team Sky had achieved their five year plan within just three years. They had not just won the Tour, they had dominated it with a Wiggins–Froome one-two finish. If they could achieve that with internal feuds broiling away, it showed how strong they really were.

In 2013 the bickering was over before the race began, with Froome the designated leader. 'Chris's Team' promoted Richie Porte to second in command and Wiggins was left home. And like Wiggins the year before, Chris Froome was untouchable. He won mountaintop finishes to Ax 3 Domaines and Mont Ventoux. He won the Stage 17 individual time trial and claimed

the yellow jersey, more than four minutes ahead of second place Nairo Quintana. For non-Sky fans the GC race was a tad dull. But for the Brit-backed team they'd just won two Tours de France in a row, and confirmed themselves as the new powerhouse of world cycling.

There was much promise for the 2014 Tour with the show down between Froome, Vincenzo Nibali (Astana) and Alberto Contador (Saxo Bank) billed as one of the best in recent years. The first true test of the leaders came on the fifth stage from Ypres to Arenberg on a stage that would feature many cobbled sectors. Unfortunately for Sky, Froome's Tour ended with the defending champion crashing twice during the sodden stage and abandoning the race before the cobbles had even begun. Scans later revealed Froome had fractured his left wrist and right hand. Team Sky's Plan B kicked in for Richie Porte, but the Tasmanian had not had an ideal run in to the race and ended the Tour in 23rd position.

It's fair to say Team Sky have been the headline team of the Tour over the past five years, but what the future holds is even more tantalising. Chris Froome and Team Sky are only just getting started, and that, is a story that will continue to be told.

TEAM SKY POWERS THROUGH THE ALPS ON STAGE 19 OF THE 2013 TOUR

TEAM SKY ON STAGE 21 OF THE 2014 TOUR DE FRANCE

ORICA-GREENEDGE:
THE UNDERDOGS FROM DOWN UNDER

DEBUTING AT THE TOUR DE FRANCE IN 2012, Orica-GreenEDGE became the first ever Australian team to take to world cycling's highest stage. Born from a phone call in 2010 between Australian businessman—and now GreenEDGE financial guarantor—Gerry Ryan and then Australian Institute of Sport High Performance Director—and now GreenEDGE General Manager—Shayne Bannan, the Orica-GreenEDGE team went from ambitious plan to reality in just two years.

The arrival of Orica-GreenEDGE as the first Australian team to take on the race was not unexpected, but if anything, overdue. In 1914 Iddo 'Snowy' Munro and Don Kirkman were the first two Australians to ride the Tour de France. In 1981 Phil Anderson became the first Australian—and non-European—to wear the race leaders' yellow jersey, a year later he also became the first Australian to win a Tour de France stage. By 2005 as many as 10 Australians were racing the Tour, and by 2011 Cadel Evans had become the first Aussie to win it. Australia deserved its own team.

GreenEDGE's first year in the WorldTour ranks was given the tick of approval worldwide. A national champion, 29 victories, and most importantly, a Spring Classic title in Milan–San Remo to Simon Gerrans meant round one was a pass. But for the fans of July, the team had come up short. Matt Goss was the team's designated sprinter, and having been labelled by Mark Cavendish as the only rider he feared could beat him in a bunch sprint, expectations were high. GreenEDGE went in chasing the green jersey and stage wins for Goss and came out with five podiums and a third place in the green jersey. This was encouraging, but not enough.

RIDERS OF ORICA GREENEDGE TEAM IN THE TIME-TRIAL, STAGE 4, OF THE 2013 TOUR DE FRANCE

TEAM ORICA GREENEDGE ON STAGE 5 OF THE 2013 TOUR

ON THE PODIUM AFTER WINNING THE 2013 TIME TRIAL

2013, however, was the Australian team's true coming of age. That year the Tour de France started on the island of Corsica and the 146km third stage from Ajaccio to Calvi had been earmarked as one for the punchy climbers. Simon Gerrans had been targeting the stage for the better part of six months and the man known as the 'Sniper' of world cycling hit his mark once again. A tremendous lead-out from Daryl Impey was capped by Gerrans who snuck home ahead of Peter Sagan (then Cannondale) in a photo finish. The excitement only increased in the following stage team time trial where Orica set the record for the fastest TTT in Tour history, 57.84km/hr over the 24.5km course, and placed Gerrans in the *maillot jaune*. Gerrans wore the jersey for Stage 5, then at the end of the Stage 6 he made the incredible decision to lose time in the final dash to the line such that his teammate Impey took the lead. Rarely seen before in professional cycling, this act of 'sharing' the lead from one teammate to another by no means de-valued the prestige of the jersey, but only enhanced the image of camaraderie and mateship within GreenEDGE.

Since its foundation GreenEDGE has grown organically, and the next step for the team is to target the GC. GreenEDGE were clear in their intent to *not* sign a Grand Tour contender in their first year. Like any new team the natural progression was to target one-day classics and Grand Tour stages before going after the biggest prize of them all. And two young riders on the team's roster: Australian Jack Haig and Columbian Esteban Chaves, provide much promise for the future. Haig is known in Australian circles as the unknown mountain biker who when invited to a training camp in Tasmania managed to out climb both Richie Porte and Nathan Earle of Team Sky. In 2011 Chaves won the Tour de l'Avenir, a race commonly referred to as the 'junior' Tour de France, and was picked up by GreenEDGE after an injury interrupted 2013. Both will require mentoring and protected development, but both present themselves as future Grand Tour contenders.

Aside from GC talent, GreenEDGE are also harbouring one of the most exciting Australians on two wheels: Caleb Ewan. Ewan burst onto the scene in 2012 at the Jayco Bay Cycling Classic where the then-17-year-old took two out of four stages. The young sprinter had out-foxed an entire GreenEDGE team on debut, and it was only fitting he join them again in 2014 to start his professional career.

Orica-GreenEDGE has made history for all the right reasons. Much like Team Sky they have captured the interest of patriotic cycling fans within their respective nations, and for those abroad they've confirmed that Australia's place on the cycling world stage is warranted. But given their talent-packed roster, the most fascinating feature of Orica-GreenEDGE is not a review of what their history has been, but predictions of what their future will be.

MOVISTAR:
THE REMAINS OF THE SPANISH ARMADA

MOVISTAR REPRESENT THE SHIFT OF POWER in world cycling. Although the Spanish team finished 2013 and 2014 as the number-one ranked nation in the world; the fact that they stand alone in 2015 as the only Spanish WorldTour— or Professional Continental—team, confirms that the Spanish talent pool is shrinking. In the zero-sum game of World Cycling, as non-traditional powers in Sky and GreenEDGE rise to the fore, it must be that those in the European stronghold face some decline. But rest assured, whilst Spanish teams and riders may be on the decrease in gross numbers, what remains is outstandingly strong.

Movistar bear their current moniker owing to team sponsor Movistar, a Spanish telecommunications company, but the team's history stretches back to its foundation in 1980. Having passed previously as Reynolds, Banesto, Iller Balears and most recently Caisse d'Epargne, the team of many titles is best remembered for the name Miguel Indurain. The five-time winner also known as 'Big Mig' won the Tour without break between 1991 and 1995, and it is his legacy that leaves the current Spanish team with high expectations.

In 2010 the Movistar trophy cabinet was decidedly bare; the team won no stages at the Tour and scrimped away with a second in the team classification. Their French climber Christophe Moreau was the runner-up in the King of the Mountains but for a team chasing victory, a runner-up is simply the first loser. In 2011, the team's sprinter Jose Joaquin Rojas finished second to Mark Cavendish in the points jersey, but it was Rui Costa's stellar breakaway win on Stage 8 that saved Movistar's Tour.

2012 was another lean year for the Spanish powerhouse with a stage win to Alejandro Valverde on the 143.5km Stage 17 from Bagnères-de-Luchon to Peyragudes providing solace. Although any team can market success from a Tour de France stage win, it was Movistar's inability to make any impact on the iron grip of the Wiggins led Team Sky that presented concern. Cycling fans, Spanish or not, were beginning to lament what appeared was a return to the dominating days of the US Postal Train in the early 00s. Team Sky's tactics of riding a constant pace for their leader with one eye on the road ahead, and another on their power meter, meant that the life was slowly being squeezed out of the race.

As the 2013 Tour de France hit the high mountains for the first time on Stage 8, such was Team Sky's evisceration of the competition that fans were considering switching off for the final two weeks. The race was only one mountain stage old and Froome and Porte had finished one-two with ease. The race appeared over.

It was the following day, however, when the excitement kicked back in. The 169km stage from Saint-Girons to Bagnères-de-Bigorre presented the Col de Portet d'Aspet, a short but punchy 5.4km climb, coming within the first 30km of racing. Movistar joined Garmin-Sharp (now Cannondale-Garmin) in an early onslaught of attacks that saw Sky reduced to just Froome and Porte with 140km and four more mountain passes to climb.

Subsequent attacks saw Porte distanced and Froome left on his own for what he later told reporters was 'was one of the hardest days I've ever had on a bike.'

Dan Martin, the Irish opportunist, took the stage for Garmin whilst Valverde—Movistar's GC leader at that time—failed to make inroads to Froome's GC lead. But Movistar did three crucial things that day. Firstly, they proved that Team Sky was beatable, that chinks existed in their black armour. Secondly, they moved Nairo Quintana into the lead of young rider's competition. Thirdly they left Porte 18 minutes in arrears which reduced Sky's one-two stranglehold, and set the stage for Quintana's eventual move into second on GC. Although a 2013 Tour de France victory for Valverde over Froome may have appeared unlikely, Movistar showed they had the strongest team and the brightest light for future editions. It was a strategic blow.

By the end of the Tour in 2013, the promise of Quintana had burgeoned to almost mystical proportions. Froome did indeed claim the Tour for Sky, but Quintana had cemented his threat. He finished second to Froome on Mont Ventoux, he won the Stage 20 hilltop finish to Annecy-Semnoz, he finished second on GC, and won the King of the Mountains *and* best young rider jerseys. Quintana was the name on everyone's lips. All at the age of 23.

For 2014 Movistar decided to continue Quintana's tutelage by sending him to the Giro d'Italia—which he won—and gave Valverde what all and sundry assume was his last chance to be dedicated leader at the Tour. With mishaps removing Froome and Alberto Contador (Tinkoff-Saxo) from the race, it presented an amazing opportunity for the ever-consistent Valverde. But no-one in 2014 was getting anywhere near eventual winner Vincenzo Nibali (Astana) with Valverde taking a career-best fourth place by the time he reached Paris.

It is abundantly clear that future Tour de France battles are set to reach a climax when Froome, Nibali, Contador and Quintana all reach the start line in July. With youth and a strong Spanish team on his side, Quintana will certainly reach the podium again. And it seems most probable that a yellow jersey will visit Columbia at least once before his career closes.

TEAM MOVISTAR PRIOR TO THE 2013 TOUR DE FRANCE

ON STAGE 3 OF THE 2013 TOUR

TINKOFF-SAXO:
RIIS AND TINKOV: PARTNERS IN CRIME

REGISTERED IN RUSSIA AND BASED IN DENMARK, Tinkoff-Saxo represents the fusion of two of cycling's biggest personalities: Russian businessman Oleg Tinkov and Danish former pro Bjarne Riis. Since 2012 Tinkov owns the team and provides sponsorship through Tinkoff Bank, his Russian credit systems company. Riis manages the team and brought on board co-sponsor Saxo Bank, a Danish investment bank.

Best known for his eccentric behaviour and possible alcohol influenced social media outbursts, Tinkov contrasts heavily with the more predictable and regimented Riis. The bottom line though, is that they produce results. It is oft said that Riis is the one team manager that a rider should *never* show up to a pre-season camp overweight for. Ruthless and uncompromising, Riis proves the perfect match for the cut-throat Tinkov.

The team can trace its roots to 1998 when a Danish team named Team Home Jack & Jones was compiled to race second division races in Europe. In 2000 Riis took over the reins and CSC (Computer Sciences Corporation) began an association with Riis and Danish cycling that included team naming-rights from 2001–08.

Riis instigated a strict militaristic philosophy within CSC that has remained with the team ever since. With the help of some friends from the Danish Army, Riis and CSC were soon renowned for their brutal pre-season camps composed of wilderness, isolation and military exercises. This legacy lives on today.

In the pre-Tinkov days, Riis guided Andy Schleck to a controversial second

THE 2014 TEAM SHOT

AND IN ACTION STAGE 3 OF THE 2013 TOUR

place behind Alberto Contador (then Astana) in 2010. The first scandal to mire that year's race was the 'Chaingate' scandal in which Contador appeared to attack knowing that Schleck had suffered a dropped chain. In the end, Contador took a slim 39-second victory GC over the Luxembourger that was later overturned when Contador returned a positive doping test for clenbuterol. Team Saxo Bank and Schleck were eventually awarded the Tour de France title, but for both it was a hollow and unglamorous victory.

In a complete about-face for 2011, Andy and Frank Schleck, Stuart O'Grady and Fabian Cancellara had all flown the Riis coop for the Luxembourg-based Leopard Trek team. Riis had, however, lured his former foe in Alberto Contador across to the team. Whilst Contador's 2011 was being overshadowed by the ongoing clenbuterol investigation, Riis took his main charger to the Giro d'Italia in case he was barred before arriving at the Tour that year. The result was a Giro victory that was later annulled, and a tired performance in July that saw Contador fading to fifth, another result later negated.

Riis and Tinkov brought Contador straight back into racing with a stunning victory in the Vuelta a España in 2012 following the completion of his suspension. Excitement for 2013 was steadily building. The 2013 tour, unfortunately for Contador, was a battle between Froome and Quintana with the Spaniard confined to an unfamiliar backseat role. Tinkoff-Saxo claimed the overall team prize, Contador was fourth on GC and Romain Kreuziger was fifth. Clearly Riis had drilled his team to an adequate level, but to take on Froome the team needed more.

And Tinkov certainly let them know. In a twitter rampage pre-Stage 12 Tinkov served up the following:

'Chris Froome is surprisingly strong. But I still in believe with Team Saxo Tinkoff and alberto Contador. Guys let's fire, go and FUCK them!'

'No mercy for SKY, From Saturday on, GO and tore them apart OR die on the road my dear Saxo Tinkov team. $$$$$$$$$'

'and remember WORLD. Russia and Tinkov Bank have been never defeated in the history. We own 30% of the World's terra. Why we give up TDF? NO!'

By Stage 13 Tinkov had seemingly accepted his defeat:

'I'm going to buy a dog, name it Froome, and will beat him up every morning and evening. Then will keep him out of food for 3 weeks.Revenge #Tdf'

Former Australian professional Nick Gates has ridden the Tour twice and worked under Tinkov as a directeur sportif with Tinkoff-Saxo. His apt summation of Tinkov and his carefree tweeting is simple; Oleg simply 'does not give a shit'.

Tinkov may not give a shit how he is perceived on social media. But such an astute businessman *does* give a shit what happens with his money, and he wants his contribution to result in Tour de France victory.

The 2014 Tour was a mixed bag for Tinkoff-Saxo. The loss of Contador was a clear hit to Riis and Tinkov, but stage wins to Michael Rogers and Rafal Majka, with the latter also pocketing a King of the Mountains jersey, meant that the tour remained a successful affair.

With Majka, Contador, Rogers and Kreuziger (pending a biological passport query at time of writing) all on board for 2015, Tinkoff-Saxo's future Tour de France hopes appear bright.

ASTANA:
THE STRUGGLE FOR POWER

SCANDAL AND DRAMA FOLLOW the Tour de France wherever it goes. It's just a reality of life that where incentives are abundant, cheating will take place. But amongst the mire of confusion and invalid results that can stain the Tour, there remain great victories for clean riders, underdogs and up-and-comers.

It is fair to say that drama has followed Astana throughout its life, but at the same time, we just can't look away. Moments of brilliance and edge-of-the seat entertainment render Astana an essential part of the Tour de France no matter ones' stance.

Spanish team Liberty Seguros-Würth faced a sponsorship void in 2006 following the Operación Puerto doping investigation and then rider Alexandre Vinokourov seized the opportunity, and instigated the formation of the Astana-Würth cycling team. Vinokourov, a Kazakh national hero, coordinated the backing of a Kazakh business consortium and the new team was born. Astana has since been the breeding ground for some of the great power struggles of recent years. 2009 was billed as the year for Alberto Contador to take Tour de France yellow under the guidance of Johan Bruyneel. But it was the return of Lance Armstrong that caused clear discomfort to the Spaniard. Contador took the victory, but the internal Astana squabbles provided ongoing drama.

Later that year, the spectacle spilled from the riders to management with the return of Alexandre Vinokourov. The founding member was set to finish a doping suspension in August of 2009 but Bruyneel was not readily seeking the Kazakh's signature. Although Bruyneel supposedly oversaw the Astana team,

'Vino' called a press conference to clarify just who ran the team.

'This team was created for me and thanks to my efforts,' Vinokourov told reporters. 'I have served my suspension and I do not see why I could not return. If Bruyneel does not want me, it will be Bruyneel who is leaving the team.'

Bruyneel and Armstrong were soon departing for Team RadioShack, and it is fair to say that conclusion has since been written.

Vinokourov moved into management after retiring in 2012 and lured the talented Vincenzo Nibali across from Liquigas. Vino and Vincenzo put their first yellow jersey in the bag with their 2014 victory, but the team remains enmeshed in scandal. One positive test for the Astana WorldTour team and four positives for Astana's Continental team in 2014 certainly casts clouds. But despite the underlying controversy, the UCI awarded Astana a WorldTour licence for 2015 with President Brian Cookson stating that Astana is 'drinking in [the] last chance saloon.'

The future for Astana at the time of writing is unclear. The team has an abundance of talent on its roster, and strong and dependable financial backing. Questions of ethics and doping investigations will be ongoing, and outcomes always arrived after the fact. Astana will be a part of the Tour de France for at least 2015. And no matter which way the tide turns, they'll be in the headlines for a while to come.

PINOT, NIBALI, SAGAN AND MAJKA ON THE PODIUM AFTER STAGE 21 OF THE 2014 TOUR

TEAM ASTANA PRIOR TO THE 2013 TOUR

CHASING ON STAGE 9 OF THE 2014 TOUR

The past five years has seen Mark Cavendish cement himself as the most successful sprinter in Tour de France history with a staggering 25 individual stage wins all before the age of 30.

But the period has also given rise to arguably the sprinter of his generation in Peter Sagan who has won three consecutive green jerseys and shows no signs of being challenged for years to come.

Germany, which produced legendary sprinter Erik Zabel who holds the record for the most points classifications in Tour history with six, has also unearthed two giants in André Greipel and Marcel Kittel, with the latter showing enough top-end speed to leave even Cavendish wanting another gear in the final of a sprint.

Kittel made an emphatic statement in 2013 when he finally ended Cavendish's unbeaten run on the traditional final stage of the Tour de France on the Champs-Elysées. Cavendish had won four from four in Paris before Kittel showed there was perhaps a new top-dog in town by out-sprinting the best in the world—a feat he repeated in 2014.

The only other sprinter besides Cavendish and Sagan to have won the points classification at the Tour in the past five years is Italian Alessandro Petacchi—who is still riding at the age of 40.

Petacchi's career again peaked in 2010 when he became the first Italian in more than 40 years to win the green jersey at the Tour de France, which also completed his hat-trick of points classifications in the three Grand Tours.

But what exactly is the ultimate measure of success for a sprinter at the Tour de France remains a point of conjecture. Stage wins don't always guarantee the points classification, as Cavendish will attest with only one green jersey from 25 stage triumphs. By contrast, Zabel only won twelve stages in total but has six green jerseys in his wardrobe. The frightening prospect is a rider who can do both, like Sagan, who has four stage wins and three green jerseys and at just 24 years of age it seems we ain't seen nothing yet.

FIVE OF THE
BEST SPRINTERS

MARK
CAVENDISH

PETER
SAGAN

MARCEL
KITTEL

ANDRE
GREIPEL

ALESSANDRO
PETACCHI

REECE HOMFRAY

MARK
CAVENDISH

MARK CAVENDISH, AFFECTIONATELY DUBBED the 'Manx Missile', earned a reputation on the road as the fastest sprinter in the world but it was on the velodrome where he developed his devastating turn of speed.

The young rider from the Isle of Man became a world champion in the Madison in 2005 and rode the track at the 2008 Beijing Olympics but it wasn't until he turned all of his attention to the road that he began to realise his true potential.

Cavendish graduated from his amateur team to turn professional with T-Mobile in 2007 and enjoyed instant success with 11 stage wins in his neo-pro season equalling the record set by fellow sprinter Petacchi.

That year he also made his Tour de France debut but had to wait another season for his maiden stage victory, which arrived in Chateauroux on Stage 5 in 2008.

That win opened the floodgates and a fortnight later Cavendish left the Tour after Stage 14 with four wins and a reputation as one of the best young sprinters in the world.

He showed top-end speed that is rarely matched and was hailed as the fastest man in the world by regularly hitting 70km/h plus in a flat finish.

Cavendish justified the hype the next year and the records started tumbling. He won six stages of the 2009 Tour de France and in doing so became the first Brit to wear the green jersey as the leader of the points classification for consecutive days, and also broke the British record for the most number of stage wins.

WINNING STAGE 11 OF THE 2011 TOUR

POWERING ON STAGE 8 OF THE 2012 TOUR

By winning on the final stage on the Champs-Elysées in Paris, Cavendish also started his run of four consecutive wins on the Tour's final day, which is a record that still stands.

The fiery sprinter showed his toughness in 2010 when he recovered from an early crash to win five stages, taking his career tally to 15, and finish second behind Petacchi in the points classification.

Despite his growing success, 2011 was somewhat of a breakthrough for the Manxman who won one-day classic Milan–San Remo, the UCI Road World Championship and finally the green jersey at the Tour de France.

That year he won twice in the first week of the Tour and took the jersey on Stage 11 which he held all the way to Paris to become the first British cyclist in history to win the points classification. Again he was unstoppable on the Champs-Elysées where he stretched his winning run to three.

The 2012 season brought about a change as Cavendish joined British super-team Sky Procycling, and despite the team's focus on delivering Bradley Wiggins to overall victory and the yellow jersey, Cavendish was still able to win three stages for himself.

But ambitions for the yellow and green jersey aren't always compatible on the same team and Cavendish left for Belgian outfit Quick Step in 2013 where he reunited with his key lead-out man in Australian Mark Renshaw and continued his winning ways. Few wins were more memorable than his 25th career victory at the Tour de France when he out-sprinted Peter Sagan in the green jersey after a breakaway on Stage 13 to Saint-Amand-Montrond.

Wearing the British national champion's jersey, Cavendish hit out with 200m to go and left his rivals in his wake as he became the third most successful rider in Tour history.

The 2014 edition of the Tour showed how fickle the sport of cycling can be as a crash in a hectic finale on Stage 1 left Cavendish with a broken collarbone and he was forced to abandon the race.

Still, with 25 stages to his name— 15 of them coming between 2010 and 2014—and all before his 30th birthday, Cavendish had already long cemented his standing as one of the sport's greats.

The emergence of sprinters like Kittel and Sagan in recent years means Cavendish now faces arguably the biggest challenge of his career to keep winning beyond the age of 30.

He might trail Bernard Hinault by three stages and Eddy Merckx by nine on the list of all-time Tour de France stage winners, but there is a good chance Cavendish will catch them by the end of his career and therefore be known not only as the greatest sprinter the Tour de France has seen but also its most prolific full stop.

PETER
SAGAN

PETER SAGAN HAS ALREADY DONE ENOUGH to be remembered as one of the greatest sprinters in history and the scary thing is his career is only just beginning.

At 25, he has won the points classification at the Tour de France three times and needs just three more to equal Erik Zabel's record for the most ever.

Sounds easy and it probably is the way Sagan has dominated the race for the green jersey in recent years.

Proof of Sagan's versatility as a rider and consistency as a sprinter is the fact that among his three consecutive green jerseys from 2012–14 are a total of just four individual stage wins.

By contrast the last man to win the green jersey before Sagan's reign was Mark Cavendish in 2011 when he won five stages in that one year alone.

In many ways Sagan has changed the face of sprinting at the Tour de France in recent years, showing an ability to match some of the world's best fast-men for pace but also get over some of the major climbs while those same rivals are fighting for survival in the grupetto.

What was once considered a prize for the sprinter with the most stage wins to his name, Sagan is rarely beaten in intermediate sprints and is as tactically brilliant as he is fast in pursuit of the green jersey.

Such is his all-round strength including an ability to time trial, the Slovak rider has even been spoken about as a possible Grand Tour contender in the future.

But Sagan has never been one to follow convention, right from his

IN ACTION ON STAGE 19 OF THE 2013 TOUR

MAJKA, PINOT, NIBALI AND SAGAN SHORTLY AFTER THE START OF THE FINAL STAGE OF THE 2014 TOUR

early days when he would ride his mountain bike in sports shoes and a T-shirt, to his entertaining and spontaneous victory salutes and wheelies in the Tour de France.

He emerged as a talented mountain bike rider and by 2008 was a junior mountain bike world champion but a road career beckoned and he turned professional in 2010 with Italian team Liquigas.

Two years later he made his Tour de France debut at the age of 22 and took just one stage to announce his arrival.

Stage 1 suited him perfectly, 198km from Liège to Seraing, with a slightly uphill finish. The young gun showed no sign of nerves but rather embraced the pressure and beat a seasoned superstar in Fabian Cancellara for a perfect Tour debut.

That day Sagan assumed the green jersey which he would wear all the way to Paris three weeks later. Along the way he picked up another win on Stage 3.

Again, Sagan proved to the world he was a force to be reckoned with after saluting on a stage which featured six categorised climbs in a tough opening week of the Tour.

Not only did he unleash his brutal sprint on the final climb of the day to the finish at Boulogne-sur-Mer, he had time to cross the line with a Forrest Gump running celebration on his bike.

The following year Sagan took until Stage 7 to record his first victory but again he already held the green jersey from Stage 3 which he protected for the duration of the race.

Stage 7 was 205.5km from Montpellier to Albi and Sagan took maximum points in the points classification at the first intermediate sprint and again at the finish thanks to the tireless work of his teammates who drove a ferocious pace on the front.

After a tough first week when he finished second on three occasions, Stage 7 was Sagan's for the taking and there was no denying him in the sprint finish.

Amazingly in 2014 Sagan again dominated the race for the green jersey and won the points classification for a third straight year, but without winning a single stage of the Tour.

Sagan was super-consistent—he finished in the top five of the first seven stages, took the green jersey on Stage 2 and never let up.

He has raced three Tours de France for a combined 63 stages and has been in green for 58 of them.

What may complicate things from 2015 onwards is his decision to switch teams to join Tinkoff-Saxo where Spanish Tour winner Alberto Contador will be targeting the yellow jersey at the same time Sagan may well want green. But as he has shown in previous years, Sagan doesn't always need support from his team as he's strong enough to go it alone.

SAGAN WINS STAGE 1 OF THE 2012 TOUR

MARCEL
KITTEL

MARCEL KITTEL IS KNOWN AS ONE of the more stylish riders in the peloton so it's no surprise that when he wins at the Tour de France, he does so in style.

Such as taking the leader's yellow jersey on the first day of the 100th edition of the race—there is no bigger statement to make than that.

Or for the past two years how he has made the Champs-Elysées, the famous shopping strip for the rich and famous in Paris, his own on the final day of the Tour.

At 188cm tall and weighing 85kg, which is heavy for a professional cyclist, Kittel cuts an imposing figure on the bike and has the trendy haircut and model looks to match.

After Mark Cavendish's five-year domination at Le Tour, Kittel is leading the next generation of sprinters of which he is arguably the biggest, strongest and fastest of the lot.

The son of a sprint cyclist father and high-jumping mother, an athletic career always beckoned the German and he turned to cycling after holidaying in the alps.

Like so many young cyclists, Kittel emerged on a mountain bike but what may surprise some who watch him dominate bunch sprints now is that he was actually a very good time triallist and in 2005 became under-23 time trial world champion.

In 2011 he turned professional with Skil-Shimano and broke Cavendish and Alessandro Petacchi's record for the most number of wins for a first-year cyclist in professional cycling with a staggering 17 victories.

WINNING STAGE 1 OF THE 2013 TOUR

The following year in 2012 and at the age of 24 Kittel was to be let loose on the Tour de France but he lasted just five days after succumbing to an intestinal infection. The cycling world would have to wait another year to see what Kittel was capable of on the biggest stage the sport has to offer.

He returned eager to make amends in 2013 which coincided with the 100th edition of the Tour de France and Kittel wasted no time making a statement.

Stage 1 was 213km from Porto-Vecchio to Bastia in Corsica and predictably it finished with a bunch sprint where he had too much speed for the likes of Alexander Kristoff who was second.

Not only did Kittel take the famous yellow jersey, known at the Tour as the *maillot jaune*, but he also took possession of the green sprinter's jersey and white jersey as the race's best young rider in what he described as the best day of his life.

That was only the beginning of a hugely successful Tour for Kittel who repeated his triumph on Stages 9, 12 and on the final day Stage 21 when he ended Cavendish's four-year run as the king of Paris.

Peter Sagan might have won the points classification in the 2013 Tour de France (Cavendish was second and André Greipel third) but Kittel left perhaps the biggest impression: there was a new king in town when it came to pure speed at the finish.

Kittel started his 2014 season in Australia at the Tour Down Under where he won the opening criterium which put him on a path to another successful season.

He returned to the Tour

ON STAGE 1 OF THE 2014 TOUR

de France where like 2013 he bookended the three-week race perfectly by winning the first and last stages and two others in between.

Enormous crowds greeted the peloton as the Tour began in Leeds in northern England and on Stage 1 Kittel gave them a thrill after local hero Cavendish crashed near the finish.

By crossing the line first, Kittel took the yellow jersey for the second year in a row and reminded everyone he again meant business.

In an amazing first week Kittel also won Stages 3 and 4, which were both sprints, before fighting his way to Paris where he again had his name in lights as the fastest man in the race.

With eight individual stage wins to his name from just two full Tours de France, Kittel is one of the most exciting riders on the WorldTour and at just 25 he's going to be around for a long time to come.

As the peloton is already discovering, it's going to take a big, strong, fast rider or one with an almighty good sprint train to beat him.

WINS STAGE 1 OF THE 2014 TOUR DE FRANCE

ANDRÉ
GREIPEL

ON HIS DAY ANDRÉ GREIPEL HAS the speed and power to beat the best sprinters in the world but it took him to leave the shadow of Mark Cavendish to fully realise it.

The big German nicknamed 'The Gorilla' for his hulking stature over the bike, Greipel has become one of the most successful sprinters of the modern era.

He has won a total of twelve stages across all three Grand Tours including six at the Tour de France between 2011 and 2014 when he joined Belgian team Lotto.

Greipel had success at under-23 level but his career really took off when he signed with the T-Mobile team and in many ways what he achieved in Australia was the making of him—or in the very least—filled him with the confidence he needed to establish himself in the professional peloton.

He won the Tour Down Under in 2008 and 2010 on his way to becoming the most successful rider in the event's history with 16 individual stage wins by the end of 2014.

But as promising as Greipel was, he had to wait for his Tour de France debut as he was on the same team as Cavendish and there was only room for one top dog sprinter on the team—and Cavendish wasn't exactly struggling for results.

Although he rode the Giro d'Italia and Vuelta a España in 2007 and 2008, he didn't go to the Tour de France until 2011 when he left HTC-Highroad to join his new Belgian squad.

WINNING STAGE 5 OF THE 2012 TOUR

On debut it didn't take long for Greipel to find himself going head to head with his former teammate. Stage 10 was 158km from Aurillac to Carmaux and finished with a bunch sprint in which Greipel confirmed that he could deliver on the big stage by beating none other than Cavendish into second place. He finished the 2011 Tour de France with four top-five finishes including third on the Champs-Elysées in Paris and aided by one of—if not the best—lead-out team in the peloton. It was just the start of Greipel's success at the biggest bike race on the planet.

He returned to the Tour in 2012 and this time on Stage 2 the tables were turned with Cavendish relegating him to second place in a frantic finish in Tournai.

But back-to-back stage wins were just around the corner. The first arrived on Stage 4 from Abbeville to Rouen when Greipel managed to avoid a late crash and then on Stage 5 to Saint-Quentin he was simply too good as Cavendish who was world champion at the time had to settle for fifth.

But his most impressive win at that year's Tour de France arguably came on Stage 13 when he had to negotiate a tricky climb late in the stage which eliminated Cavendish from contention.

Once again the strength of Greipel's team helped put him in a perfect position by chasing down a two-man breakaway who escaped after the climb on Mont Saint Clair and the big sprinter was able to finish the job by beating Peter Sagan on the line.

There would be two more stage wins for Greipel in the next two editions of the Tour de France. The first arrived on Stage 6 in 2013 when he won in typically commanding style by launching a perfectly timed sprint to beat Sagan and fellow German Marcel Kittel who was becoming a force in his own right at the Tour.

Greipel returned to the race in 2014 where Stage 6 was again his lucky number. After a tough opening five stages in which he finished in the top ten only once, Greipel hit back in a big way by winning the 194km trek from Arras to Reims.

He went to the front inside the final 150m and despite a flurry of late attacks from his rivals Greipel crossed the line more than one bike length in front to take his career tally of Tour de France stage wins to six.

With the emergence of Kittel and Sagan in recent years, and as long as Cavendish keeps riding, Greipel is going to have to fight all the way to add to his collection of Tour victories.

At 32 he is the oldest of the quartet by at least three years and while he's not over the hill, he's probably not getting any faster either.

But if Greipel's career was to stop tomorrow, he would still be remembered as one of the great sprinters of his generation.

ANOTHER WIN: STAGE 10 OF THE 2011 TOUR

AND AGAIN, WINNING STAGE 6 OF THE 2014 TOUR

ALESSANDRO
PETACCHI

ALESSANDRO PETACCHI IS AN ITALIAN SPRINTER whose career is characterised by his longevity in the sport as much as it is by his speed at the finish of a bike race.

At the end of 2014 he had won a whopping 48 Grand Tour stages, mostly at the Giro d'Italia and Vuelta a España, but also six at the Tour de France including the 2010 green jersey as winner of the points classification.

His days of winning might be over but Petacchi remained in the WorldTour peloton until the end of the 2014 season where he rode mostly as a lead-out man for Mark Cavendish at the Quick Step team.

Petacchi turned professional in 1996 at the age of 22 and four years later made his Grand Tour debut where he won two stages of the Vuelta.

His Tour de France debut came a year later in 2001 when riding for Fassa Bortolo he had three top-five placings but no victory.

His maiden Tour stage win came in 2003 when Petacchi enjoyed his most successful Tour with four stage victories in the first eight days before abandoning the race as it headed for the mountains.

Petacchi won Stages 2, 4, 6 and 7 and briefly wore the green jersey before calling an end to his Tour with two weeks still to go and the roads starting to go upwards.

He would switch teams three times between 2005 and 2010 and was hit with a doping ban which saw him stripped of results in the 2007 Giro d'Italia and miss that year's Tour de France, which he did not race again until 2010.

In 2010 Petacchi signed with Italian team Lampre and so began his quest

PETACCHI ...

... WINNING

... STAGE 4 OF THE TOUR

to win the green jersey at the Tour, which would complete the hat-trick of points classifications after his previous achievements in the Giro and Vuelta.

Petacchi showed that the secret to winning the points classification is not necessarily amassing stage wins, although they certainly help, but consistency throughout the whole three weeks.

Six years after he last rode the Tour de France and seven years after he won four stages, Petacchi returned in 2010 and struck on Stage 1 by winning the opening 224km trip from Rotterdam to Brussels. He had to avoid three crashes in the closing 3km which eliminated some of his biggest rivals but still had the speed to beat those left standing when it mattered.

That win put him in the green jersey, but for the following stage only, as he would not see it again until Stage 11.

However he didn't have to wait that long for a second stage win at that year's Tour as he again won on Stage 4 from Cambrai to Reims.

Having caught the breakaway late in the stage, the sprinters' teams started lining up but it was Petacchi at the age of 36 who proved there

was still plenty of fight left in him when he took line honours.

Petacchi would not win another stage for the rest of the Tour yet he rode into Paris on the final day in the green jersey to complete a hugely successful three weeks.

The green jersey changed hands between he and Thor Hushovd five times in the final ten days of the race but Petacchi collected five top-five finishes in that time to put enough points on the board to be in green when it mattered.

He finished the Tour with good legs as he was second in Paris on the final day behind Cavendish on the way to becoming the first Italian in 42 years to win the Tour's green jersey.

Petacchi's career spanned two generations—the early 2000s when he raced the likes of Erik Zabel—and the late 2000s when he found himself going head-to-head with, and then a teammate of, Cavendish.

With his trademark explosiveness, Petacchi was able to win stages of the Tour de France seven years apart and is one of only three men to win the Tour de France's points classification between 2010–14, and he did so at the ripe old age of 36.

IN GREEN ON STAGE 20 OF THE 2010 TOUR

It's the Michelin-starred chefs who get made judges on *Masterchef* and become celebrities in their own right. But where would they be without their own sous-chefs, vegetable-chopping apprentices, dogsbody juniors and dish washers? And what of the maître d', waiters and sommelier, without whom guests would lack both wine and a table?

Cycling's status as an individual sport contested by teams has long been one of its great paradoxes — but it wasn't always the case. In the early twentieth century riders rode only for themselves. When, in 1911, one chap offered his services to another rider, pacing him to the finish line to avoid elimination, he was savagely attacked by the Tour's organiser and chief judge. 'He is unworthy,' Henri Desgrange said of Maurice Brocco. 'He is no more than a domestique.' And so the term was coined: first as an insult, but in time — as the role became more specialised — as a form of praise.

Nowadays, cycling is very much a collaborative effort. All top riders and sprinters need domestiques. It is universally accepted, for example, that Mark Cavendish wouldn't have been so prolific in his early days were it not for his ubiquitous wingman Mark Renshaw. Sacrificing his own ambitions, a typical domestique will work pretty much entirely for the benefit of his team's protected rider(s). 'Gregario', the Italian equivalent, refers to a soldier in the Roman legions, while the Belgians and Dutch say 'knecht', which translates as 'knight'. Both are less sedentary or seemingly pejorative as domestique, the French term for a servant or butler.

Key domestique duties include pacing and protecting designated riders from the wind, chasing down breaks or thwarting attacks from rival riders and teams, fetching food and water for team-mates, swapping bikes and wheels if necessary; positioning at key moments and leading out sprinters for the stage win. In his book *Domestique*, Charly Wegelius, now a directeur sportif at Garmin-Sharp following a winless eleven-year career dedicated to serving others, describes himself as a 'hired help'.

Just as there are numerous aspects of being a domestique, there are wholly varying levels of domestique-dom: at one end there's riders burying themselves from the outset of a stage before the TV cameras are even rolling; at the other end of the spectrum is found the domestique de luxe — a star rider who could feasibly win the race himself but who has agreed to work in the interests of another. Greg LeMond carried out such duties for Bernard Hinault in 1985 en route to finishing second behind the Frenchman in Paris; a year later, their roles reversed, the American topped the podium with Hinault by his side. One of the best examples of a super-domestique in the past five years is Chris Froome, who worked selflessly to ensure Bradley Wiggins was crowned Britain's first Tour winner before usurping the king (or knight, as Sir Wiggo had become) to taste glory himself one year later.

FIVE OF THE BEST
TOUR DOMESTIQUES

MANUEL QUINZIATO   SERGIO PAULINHO   RAMUNAS
NAVARDAUSKAS   LARS BAK   KOEN DE KORT

FELIX LOWE

MANUEL
QUINZIATO

THE CHISELLED ITALIAN joined BMC from Liquigas in 2011 as a time trial and one-day specialist before transforming himself into one of the best road captains in the business. Powerful, easy on the eye, perpetually smiling and immensely likeable, Quinziato quickly established himself as Cadel Evans's most loyal domestique, and alongside George Hincapie, Marcus Burghardt and Michael Schär, formed the engine room behind the Australian's overall victory in 2011.

Ask any top Tour rider in the peloton who they would pick in a dream team and many would opt for Quinziato—a rider entirely devoid of showmanship or ego, whose reliability (he has finished all eight of his Tours to date), stealth (his highest finish was seventy-ninth), strength and positivity is universally appreciated, making him very much the domestique's domestique. A team player who acts as a big brother to many of BMC's younger riders, 'Quincy' also boasts the levelheadedness to study for a law degree during the off-season at Trento University.

In a newspaper column during Evans's victorious Tour, Quinziato described his principal role as 'making sure [our] leader is in the right place' and anticipating the crosswinds that 'can lead to a tricky situation'. He explained how he used his experience in the often wet and windy Belgian one-day races to ensure that Evans kept out of trouble during the Tour's testing opening week in Brittany. 'Who better than us, solid 80 kilo "spring classics" riders, to do the work to keep the team leader safe?' he mused.

So effective was Quinziato that Evans once admitted that it was the Italian

QUINZIATO RIDES ALONE DURING STAGE 17 OF THE 2013 TOUR

over anyone else who had the 'biggest influence on my results'. When the Australian decided to forego the Tour to race the Giro in 2014, Quinziato's name was first alongside his on the team sheet. So while Quinziato was present in BMC's Tour squad when Tejay van Garderen finished fifth and Evans seventh in 2013, he was recovering ahead of the Vuelta, and not riding his ninth Tour, when the American secured another top five finish in 2014. Present on both occasions—and in every Tour since joining BMC in 2010—was German powerhouse Marcus Burghardt, another

dependable road captain.

I'll admit, it was a hard decision to pick one over the other for this list—so hard that I even asked Manuel for his input. His reply was pretty classy: 'Do you know that a judge is not allowed to decide over a question on which he has interest? If I had to choose a domestique for myself, Burghy would be for sure my first choice.' So, how to pick between the two—taking into account Burghardt's immense capacity on the flat and his powerful engine in the foothills of the high mountains?

Well, Quinziato's relationship with Evans helped—but there's

also his famous popularity among his team-mates (he is supposedly followed by 25 BMC riders on Twitter, compared to Burghardt's 21). He's such an influential figure on the team bus that it's Quinziato, a keen music lover, who is always in charge of BMC's playlist. He is even said to have a favourite song for every occasion. 'For the hardest stages or for when I want to catch the breakaway, Rage Against The Machine is a must,' he once said. Sorry Marcus, but that sealed it for me.

DUMOULIN CHECKS ON QUINZIATO DURING THEIR BREAKAWAY ON STAGE 5 OF THE 2006 TOUR

QUINZIATO CHASING ON STAGE 7 OF THE 2011 TOUR

SERGIO
PAULINHO

SANCHO PANZA TO ALBERTO CONTADOR'S DON QUIXOTE, Portuguese all-rounder Sergio Paulinho has finished all but one of his thirteen Grand Tours to date and has been one of the Spaniard's trusty 'escudeiros'—or squires—since their time together under Manolo Saiz at Liberty Seguros. Their paths only diverged when Paulinho followed the soon-to-be-disgraced directeur sportif Johan Bruyneel to RadioShack from Astana in 2010. Previously, Paulinho had ridden alongside Contador for six years and had ably supported his friend during his Tour victories in 2007 and 2009.

Paulinho's switch to RadioShack raised eyebrows: he was Contador's room-mate and confident during the particular stressful 2009 Tour in which the champion-elect's every move was undermined by Bruyneel and Lance Armstrong. During a psychologically damaging period for Contador, Paulinho had been his only loyal domestique, burying himself in the mountains while the likes of Andreas Klöden, Yaroslav Popovych and Haimar Zubeldia all pulled strings for the Armstrong–Bruyneel axis. However context is needed: the future of Astana was up in the air and under-contract Contador was the only rider in the nine-man Tour squad who didn't jump ship with most of the team management and join RadioShack.

Alongside the likes of Benjamin Noval, Jesus Hernandez and Dani Navarro, Paulinho has been one of Contador's most trusted team-mates over the years. So much so that many even suggested he joined RadioShack to act as some kind of mole for his ally. In truth, it was probably merely a question of economics, and when Armstrong predictably fell by the wayside after crashing

PAULINHO LEADS DISCOVERY CHANNEL ON STAGE 17 OF THE 2007 TOUR

AND LEADING ASTANA ON STAGE 7 OF THE 2009 TOUR

WINNING STAGE 10 OF THE 2010 TOUR

early in the Alps of the 2010 Tour, Paulinho saved face for his new employers by riding to a memorable stage victory in Gap on Bastille Day. The Portuguese rated the win above his 2004 Olympic road race silver medal.

When RadioShack folded a year later, Paulinho was reunited with Contador by Bjarne Riis at Saxo Bank. 'For me, Alberto is the best rider in the world and the chance to work again with him is very good for me,' Paulinho said. But Contador's clenbuterol case still loomed large— when the Spaniard was eventually banned, Paulinho rode a fourth consecutive Tour, but hampered by illness and in support of Danish climber Chris Anker Sørensen, who finished fourteenth. Contador's retrospective ban ended ahead of the 2012 Vuelta and for a second

time Paulinho helped Contador to a victory in his national stage race.

Paulinho, Noval and Hernandez were all integral parts of Saxo-Tinkoff's 2013 squad when Contador made his Tour comeback, finishing fourth after tapering during the final week. When Hernandez crashed out of Stage 6 of the 2014 Tour, Paulinho's role looked all the more essential for a revitalised Contador. But it was never to be, the Spaniard himself withdrawing four days later after fracturing his tibia on a wet descent in the Vosges mountains. Having recovered in record time, Contador once again called on Paulinho's services in Spain as he beat rival Chris Froome to a third Vuelta crown.

Although Paulinho's second stint as Contador's lieutenant has not yielded as much success on the Tour

as their first period together, two Vuelta victories show that the pairing is still highly effective. Riis clearly thinks so too, prolonging Paulinho's contract until 2016. Charly Wegelius, author of *Domestique*, also shares Riis's high opinion of the 35-year-old: when I asked the Garmin-Sharp directeur sportif for his five best Tour domestiques, the Portuguese topped the list.

With Tinkoff-Saxo now possessing the Tour's reigning green jersey (Peter Sagan) and polka dot jersey (Rafal Majka), competition for places will be fiercer than ever in 2015. But you sense that Contador will seek Paulinho's steely presence as he bids to add a third yellow jersey to the two previous Tour triumphs achieved alongside the unflagging Portuguese. If selected, Paulinho will be riding his seventh Tour in eight years.

RAMUNAS
NAVARDAUSKAS

BEFORE ANDREW TALANSKY—fresh from winning the Dauphiné—spearheaded Garmin-Sharp's squad for the 2014 Tour, Jonathan Vaughters's team posted a video on YouTube in which Ramunas Navardauskas and Jack Bauer talked about one another's strengths. Fresh-faced Navardauskas was described by Bauer as 'the best team-mate that we have on the team'. The New Zealander jokingly added that Navardauskas would look after Talansky 'on the flat stages, in the mountains, on the cobbles and on the descents' while 'winning two stages minimum' and 'keeping everyone happy'.

Funnily enough, Bauer's facetious predictions weren't far off the mark: the Lithuanian powerhouse fastidiously chaperoned Talansky during the opening ten days of the race, and when the American was forced to retire through injury, expertly soloed to a stage win of his own. Far from a fluke, Navardauskas's victory in Bergerac was the culmination of a well-crafted move by Garmin, with Bauer, Sebastian Langeveld and Tom-Jelte Slagter all teeing up Navardauskas's attack on a punchy climb near the finish. There was certainly poetic justice in the consummate team player benefiting from the helping hands of those whose interests he constantly puts ahead of his own.

Navardauskas's tireless work ethic is, in fact, something his directeur sportif feels holds him back. 'We have to fight with him not to be the first guy to bring rain jackets to the car and go and get bidons,' said Charly Wegelius after his Stage 19 victory. 'Even on a day when we ask him to do the race, he's doing all the jobs for everyone else. It's a battle with him but hopefully he'll get a bit more selfish now because he's just a little bit too kind. It's going to be a problem for the peloton when he starts to realise how strong he is.'

It seems that that day will come sooner rather than later. Navardauskas had always possessed the clichéd powerful engine that makes riders of his ilk so effective. Having become a national road champion in his first year at Garmin, Navardauskas, supporting Tom Danielson and Ryder Hesjedal, finished his first Tour in fifty-fifth place in 2011—impressive for a 23-year-old neo-pro. Danielson and Hesjedal finished ninth and eighteenth respectively. Navardauskas was a key component of the Argyle Armada team behind Hesjedal's winning Giro d'Italia performance in 2012 before riding his first Giro–Tour double in support of the Canadian in 2013. Both ended miserably for Hesjedal: a nasty crash saw him retire in Italy before a broken rib sustained in the Tour's opening stage in Corsica effectively ended his chances in France.

But for Navardauskas, 2013 was a breakthrough year: he became the first Lithuanian to wear the Giro's pink jersey before helping Talansky to a top-ten Tour finish. It was these performances that prompted Vaughters to make the difficult decision of picking youth in favour of experience for the 2014 *Grand Départ* in Yorkshire, depriving British veteran David Millar the chance to ride the Tour on home soil in his final year as a pro. And yet it did not take until his solo win in Bergerac for the decision to be vindicated: from the outset, Navardauskas was a rock for Talansky, and nowhere more evident than the treacherous roads

ON STAGE 5 OF THE 2014 TOUR

ESCAPING ON STAGE 19 OF THE 2014 TOUR

of the Peak District.

Displaying the kind of temper and predatory instincts of the honey badger after which he earned his comical nickname, Navardauskas rode on the front of the peloton to shield Talansky from the baying masses, swatting a series of smart phones out of the hands of over-eager spectators on the bustling ascent of Holme Moss. Not only did he prove himself to be one of the peloton's hardest workers, Navardauskas showed his sprinting credentials with a raft of strong performances alongside the peloton's fast men. Bookending his Tour with third places in Harrogate and the Champs-Élysées, Navardauskas posted four top tens in total, often bettering the likes of André Greipel and Peter Sagan for speed.

His name may be a mouthful, but it's becoming a household one following a stellar 2014. Only 27, Navardauskas already has stage wins to his name in both the Tour and the Giro and has yet to ride the Vuelta. Until now, he has shunned the spring classics on the grounds that he finds them too stressful. But boasting similar attributes as an early Fabian Cancellara, you sense that Vaughters will try and talk Navardauskas into changing his outlook in the years to come. Either way, his status as one of the Tour's best current domestiques is undebatable. Soon, the prefix 'super' will be needed, elevating the Honey Badger to Tony Martin levels of rounded gregario-ness. Become less 'kind' and Navardauskas could well morph into a whole different kind of monster.

KITTEL STEALS STAGE 21 FROM KRISTOFF AND NAVARDAUSKAS IN 2014

LARS
BAK

'DON'T PRAISE ME,' Mark Cavendish said after his fourth-stage win of the 2011 Tour at Montpellier. 'I just had to ride the final two-hundred metres. Praise Danny Pate and Lars Bak—they rode two hundred kilometres today working for me.' Of those two men commended by the most decorated Tour sprinter of all time, Denmark's Bak stands out for his outstanding contribution to team riding over the past five years. In fact, using football's goal-assists statistics, Bak unofficially ranked the best domestique of 2011 after contributing to more wins—twenty—than anyone else in the pro peloton. Second, with 16 'assists', was Belgian Jurgen Roelandts, whom Bak would join for the 2012 season at Lotto following the dissolution of HTC-Highroad.

Strong, powerful and consistent, Lars Bak is the perfect team rider who gives 100 per cent from start to finish. A triple national time-trial champion and 2005 road race champion, the tall Dane is also capable of taming the cobbles of northern France (he finished fifth in Paris–Roubaix in 2011). Yet despite his domestic success, it is as a successful domestique that Bak will be remembered—whether in the service of sprinters Cavendish or André Greipel, or Lotto's perennial GC contender Jurgen van den Broeck.

In his wonderful book *Vélo*, essayist Paul Fournel describes the ideal rouleur—a rider who can relentlessly eat up the kilometres over demanding terrain—as possessing 'long-lasting majesty' and 'a statuesque position'. Fournel continues: 'He manages the wind like a bass manages the sea. He rides gears as heavy as anvils while having the elegance never to show it.' Bak is very much the Fournelian rouleur incarnate. His primary role is to

SPEEDING INTO STAGE 13 OF THE 2013 TOUR DE FRANCE

subjugate the peloton to his control and help manage the time gap to the breakaway, making sure it's closed neither too late nor too soon, while preventing counter-attacks before setting up the sprint finish. It was his deft showing in Paris–Roubaix in 2011 that earned Bak, aged 31, a surprisingly late maiden call-up to the Tour that year. He's been part of the furniture ever since.

Cavendish's victory on the Champs-Élysées in 2011 increased his tally to five stages—and Bak was an integral part of what was dubbed

the world's greatest lead-out train. 'Lars is just so solid,' Daniel Lloyd— himself a workhorse for Carlos Sastre during the 2010 Tour—told me when I quizzed the former Cervélo rider. 'Back in the HTC days he would ride all day on the front for Cav during the Tour. It's a very hard thing to do, and super impressive.' That year, Bak raced 102 days in total, covering 17,303km—more than any other rider according to his team. Along with pulling the peloton for most of the three weeks, helping HTC to fourth in the team

time trial and placing thirty-sixth in the penultimate day's individual time trial, Bak still had the legs to get into a break on the Champs-Élysées. Making sure that no one else in the five-man break succeeded, Bak was last to be caught by his own team's train, before slipping in to help lead out Cavendish for the win—and Britain's first ever green jersey in Paris. The expression 'hard as nails' comes to mind.

It was these kinds of Herculean performances that earned Bak the top road rider and team rider prizes

LEADING THE PELOTON ON STAGE 6 OF THE 2011 TOUR

at the Danish Bike Awards—mighty impressive for someone without a solitary victory to his name in 2011. Bak's record of riding both the Giro and the Tour every year since 2011 is not as monumental as Adam Hansen's ongoing series of Grand Tours since joining Lotto at the same time as Bak. But the Dane's overall Tour contribution is perhaps far greater, given his tendency to pick up the buck from the outset of every stage and put aside his personal ambitions in order to work for others. So far, Bak has helped

Greipel to five sprint victories on the Tour (three in 2012 and one apiece in 2013 and 2014). Were his daily kilometre-gobbling efforts followed up with the same kind of zeal by his team-mates in the closing moments of each flat stage (the Lotto train has had a tendency to derail somewhat frequently in recent years) then that total would be far more notable.

Regardless, the big cheeses at Lotto are more than happy with Bak's contribution, having tied down the 35-year-old's services until 2016. 'I presume I got this contract

extension thanks to my way of cycling, because I always try to think at the importance of the team. The team management probably knows after three years how to use me. I will give it all to play my role in the team as good as possible for the next two years.' With Greipel's star seemingly on the wane, Bak's role may differ in the years to come. Perhaps, like Hansen, he will start to fight more often for wins of his own to add to his solitary scalp from the 2012 Giro d'Italia.

KOEN
DE KORT

WHEN I TOLD A FORMER BRITISH PRO that I was going to include Bernhard
Eisel as my fifth domestique there was a (virtual) sharp intake of breath. 'Eisel
sells himself very well but others do the job better with much less fuss,' he
admonished, without further e-mail elaboration. Such scathing words were
a sledgehammer blow to the stomach. Was Bernie, with his iron jaw, perfect
stubble and quirky Austro-Australian accent, really just a drama queen?

I had just finished reading Richard Moore's enthralling *Étape*, one chapter
of which delves into the story behind Mark Cavendish's self-proclaimed
hardest day on a bike. It's the sweltering Stage 15 of the 2010 Tour de France.
Cavendish is ill and dropped by the gruppetto on each of the four major
climbs. On the third, the fearsome Col du Tourmalet, he curses his ever-
loyal HTC team-mate Eisel, whose job it is to nurse his charge through the
mountains as well as lead him out in the sprints.

The pair bicker and sulk 'like a married couple' before—in a flurry of
expletives—resolving to riding up on opposite sides of the road. It's not until
Cavendish offers Eisel a conciliatory can of Coke near the summit that they
bury the hatchet and concentrate on the task in hand: avoiding the time cut.
Together, they fight back on the descent before being distanced once again
on the Aubisque. Even gradient-wary Italian Alessandro Petacchi is ahead.
But Eisel ensures that they rejoin the gruppetto on the flat run into Pau. The
thirty-five-minute deficit is large but within the limit. After a much-needed
rest day, the pair battle the Tourmalet once again. Cavendish has a fever. He's
still under the weather and a wheezing wreck when, a day later, he sprints

to victory in Bordeaux after some expert piloting from Eisel.

Two days later, another win on the Champs-Élysées took Cavendish's tally up to five for the race. With Bernie by his side, the Manxman repeated this feat in the 2011 Tour before seizing the rainbow stripes in Copenhagen. When HTC folded, the world champion took Eisel with him to Sky where, despite a frustrating season, Cavendish still notched three wins as team-mate Bradley Wiggins won the 2012 Tour. Eisel even put in numerous shifts for Team GB on Box Hill during the Olympic road race but the gold medal eluded Cavendish. The London 2012 disappointment and fall-out from Sky marked the end an era: Cav and Bernie finally split up and the latter's influence as a domestique was curtailed.

Without a top sprinter to guide, Eisel was no longer needed as Sky put all their eggs in Chris Froome's pannier for the 2013 Tour. The addition of cobblestones to the 2014 route meant a restoration to the squad, Eisel having two Paris-Roubaix top tens to his name. But Froome's withdrawal during the dramatic fifth stage—plus the absence of both a sprinter or a bona fide Plan B—made Eisel's presence largely redundant in his tenth Tour. As one domestique's authority on the world's biggest bike race dwindled, another's grew. Enter the ring, Koen de Kort, a rider whose battling qualities are mirrored by the flamboyantly tattooed tiger and giant gladiators that adorn his back (and expose his adopted Aussie status).

While Cavendish was coming to terms with having just one designated helper assigned to him at Sky, a rising sprint star from Germany—himself with an entire team dedicated to his services—was struggling with illness. Marcel Kittel had signalled his arrival on the scene with a stage victory in the 2011 Vuelta. Rangy Dutchman de Kort was the Argos-Shimano team captain in Spain and his Pro-Continental team had high hopes when they were selected as wildcards for the 2012 Tour.

But an off-colour Kittel was forced to quit the race in the opening week after a string of pained performances. Undeterred, the Dutch team came back stronger in the Vuelta with de Kort helping John Degenkolb to five resounding victories. De Kort was yet again present as the young German added another scalp in the Giro after Argos-Shimano were granted WorldTour status. And yet, after his inauspicious introduction to the Tour a year earlier, few foresaw the impact Kittel was about to make on cycling's biggest stage.

Four sprint wins in two successive years on the Tour has made Kittel a superstar. Marshalled by de Kort, Kittel's expert sprint train has proved itself the most professional and effective since the days of Eisel et al at HTC. (What's more, de Kort's perfect Australian accent puts Eisel's confused twang to shame). Those fans who expected Cavendish to wear yellow in Corsica and in Yorkshire instead saw Kittel steal the show. Having ended Cavendish's seemingly interminable run in Paris in 2013, Kittel has also now made the Champs-Élysées his own stomping ground for two successive years.

De Kort's role in both Kittel and Degenkolb's successes cannot be overestimated. Vastly experienced and a fast finisher in his own right, the 32-year-old has built a career around helping others while establishing himself as one of the best lead-out riders in the business. You only have to watch his exhilarating on-bike footage from the 2014 Tour of California to appreciate the lengths—and perils—he goes to slingshot his men to victory.

With such a wealth of options to choose from, Giant-Shimano had two sprint train formations during the 2014 Tour: Kittel for the flat pure sprints and Degenkolb spearheading the lumpier power sprints. De Kort's role as 'speed pilot' for Kittel involved providing the first major injection of pace ahead of the *flamme rouge*, while for Degenkolb he assumed his traditional duties as final lead-out man (two second places were followed by four outright wins for Degenkolb on the Vuelta).

Eisel and Cavendish clearly ruled

the roost between 2008 and 2011 when they recorded twenty victories in four successive Tours. But Giant-Alpecin are the natural heirs to HTC's throne. And if Cav and Bernie are the past, then Kittel and de Kort are very much the present and the future of bunch sprint riding. Until Warren Barguil makes the step up and Giant-Alpecin have to accommodate a veritable GC rider within their fast-moving ranks.

DE KORT ON STAGE 6 OF THE 2012 TOUR

DE KORT AND DEGENKOLB CELEBRATE TEAMMATE KITTEL'S WIN OF STAGE 10 OF THE 2013 TOUR

Everyone knows about the achievements of Chris Froome, Bradley Wiggins and Mark Cavendish at the Tour de France, but, as that talented trio would all happily acknowledge, they've had a supporting cast of dozens of equally talented British riders by their side to help them reach the level they have.

These often unsung heroes could win — often do win — for themselves, but have carved out a niche, and indeed careers, by helping others at big races like the Tour.

But now, thanks to Froome and Wiggins's Tour titles, and Cavendish's 25-and-counting Tour stage wins, suddenly even those British riders who aren't considered the big stars — or at least not yet — are very much in demand from foreign teams keen to take advantage of a nation very much at the forefront of professional bike racing.

Many are products of the lottery-funded British Cycling Federation, whose development programmes serve to identify cycling talent early and nurture them in the hope of producing future road and track stars. Geraint Thomas and Peter Kennaugh, both at Team Sky, and Steve Cummings — a former Sky man who joined the South African MTN-Qhubeka team for 2015 — have all come through that system, as has young Simon Yates who, courted by Team Sky, was whipped from right under their noses by the Australian Orica-GreenEDGE outfit and put straight into their starting line-up for the Tour de France — a 'ready-made' elite athlete.

Others, like Froome and the now-retired David Millar, blazed their own trails as young riders, but would fall into the British system for events contested by national teams further down the line and benefit from a well-established regimen in which they could feed off their counterparts, and, in Froome's case, join the fledgling Team Sky, with the road team indirectly growing off the back of GB's Olympic track success.

Success as a nation has fully justified the generous funding from the National Lottery, without which British Cycling — and British cycling; small 'c' — would still have been stuck in the dark ages.

BRITISH RIDERS

GERAINT
THOMAS

DAVID
MILLAR

PETER
KENNAUGH

STEVE
CUMMINGS

SIMON
YATES

ELLIS BACON

GERAINT
THOMAS

HEADING INTO THE 2015 CYCLING SEASON, Commonwealth Games road-race champion Geraint Thomas was a veteran of five Tours de France. Like many of British Cycling's current generation, his background is as a track racer, and he has two Olympic titles to his name, won in the team pursuit at the 2008 and 2012 Games.

Making it a hat-trick of track gold medals in Rio de Janeiro in 2016 is unlikely, however, as Thomas has expressed his desire to see just how far he can go on the road. And while Bradley Wiggins will go back to his track roots at the Games in Brazil, there are whispers in some quarters that Thomas is capable of 'doing a Wiggins' and becoming a bona fide Tour contender in the years to come.

After his first Tour, riding for the Barloworld team, in 2007—where he was the youngest rider in the race, at 21, but stayed the course to finish second to last in Paris—Thomas didn't ride the race again until 2010, when he did so as part of Team Sky. Since then, he's ridden the Tour each year, save for in 2012 when he made himself unavailable for selection in order to concentrate on the track.

A true all-rounder—a dependable work-horse, capable of sprint lead-out duties, but also of riding well in hilly stages—Thomas was the last man to lead Cavendish into the mêlée of the final sprint at the 2011 road-race world championships, which Cavendish won, while, at the Tour, Thomas has tended to be tasked with doing whatever Sky has needed him to do.

But at the 2011 Tour, Thomas gave fans a possible glimpse of the future

as he found his climbing legs after having been given the green light to show what he could do after the team had lost Wiggins to a crash in the first week.

On Stage 12, from Cugnaux to the summit finish at Luz-Ardiden in the Pyrenees, Thomas spent a long—200km long—day in the saddle, first as part of a six-man breakaway group, and later with only Jérémy Roy of the French FDJ team for company as the pair pushed on alone.

On a tough mountain stage that included the fearsome Col du Tourmalet—the most-used mountain in the Tour—Thomas and Roy eventually ran out of steam on the final climb up to the finish and were swept up with less than 10km to go. But Thomas had showed a number of more established climbers what he was capable of on a good day.

At the 2013 Tour, 'G', as he's known within the British and Sky set-ups, joined the list of the race's most

stoic riders when he crashed on the opening stage in Corsica, fracturing his pelvis. While most people would see that as a sign to pack their bags and head home, Thomas rode on through the pain and discomfort to play his part in helping safely deliver Froome to Tour victory.

At the 2014 edition, like in 2011, Sky again lost their team leader to a crash early on—this time Froome—and the focus switched to 'alternative' leader Richie Porte after Bradley Wiggins had been left at home.

Once it became clear that the Tasmanian wasn't going well enough to challenge for the Tour title, Thomas and the team's Spanish climber, Mikel Nieve, were freed up to ride their own races, although by then it was a little too late for Thomas to truly shine.

The Welshman nevertheless managed an admirable 22nd place overall—a place ahead of Porte—

while Nieve emerged to finish as the highest-placed Sky rider, in 18th, over three-quarters of an hour down on overall winner Vincenzo Nibali of Italy.

Cardiff-born Thomas appears to be extremely well-liked within the team— a well-rounded rider and individual who knows exactly what's expected of him at any given moment, and it's perhaps those traits that could be translated into a Tour-winning mentality.

Signing a new contract with Sky during the 2014 Tour to keep him at the team until the end of 2016 suggests that Thomas has no doubts that the British set-up is the ideal environment at which to continue his development.

The question, as he seemingly leaves the track behind for good, is: just how far can Thomas go in a race like the Tour?

THOMAS AGAIN ON STAGE 5

LEADING AN ESCAPE ON STAGE 14 OF THE 2014 TOUR

DAVID
MILLAR

DAVID MILLAR'S CAREER HAS TRULY BEEN one of two halves—split by two years in the wilderness serving a doping ban.

Millar returned from that ban a changed man: contrite following his use of the illegal blood-boosting drug EPO, and ready and willing to do everything in his power to combat the scourge of doping in professional sport.

That included joining the World Anti-Doping Agency's (WADA) Athletes Committee, and he became, and remained, the go-to guy every time another doping scandal broke, always speaking eloquently and honestly about the subject.

Millar returned to competition in 2006 with the Spanish Saunier Duval team, and went straight into that year's Tour de France—his fifth since making his debut in 2000 when, at 23 years old, he'd won the race's opening time trial and wore the famous yellow jersey as leader of the race the next day.

In 2007, the Tour started in London, and on Stage 1 between the capital and Canterbury, Millar went on the attack, doing enough on the handful of categorised climbs before he was pegged back by the peloton to take the famous polka-dot 'King of the Mountains' jersey, synonymous (at least for British fans) with Robert Millar—no relation, but also Scottish—who remains the only British rider to have won the mountains classification outright, as opposed to just for a couple of days as Millar did.

Millar was no climber, but neither was he any longer 'just' the time-trial specialist or a youngster tagged as a 'potential champion'. Having hit his 30s since coming back from his ban, he raced for the pleasure of racing, and at

KITTEL SPRINTS WITH MILLAR ON STAGE 1 OF THE 2013 TOUR

MILLAR WINS STAGE 12 OF THE 2012 TOUR

AND LATER ON STAGE 19

the 2009 Tour his metamorphosis appeared complete as he again threw caution to the wind on Stage 6 from Girona into Barcelona, which saw him almost hold off the chasing peloton for the stage win, only to be swallowed up inside the final kilometre.

The attitude of those who thought they'd never be able to forgive him for doping had begun to change, too, and almost everyone was rooting for him on Stage 9 of the 2010 Tour de France, which he calls his toughest ever day on the bike.

Millar had crashed multiple times on Stage 2, and had struggled through the first week with his injuries. Despite the rest day after Stage 8, Millar was battered and bruised all over, and ideally would have preferred another day in bed.

Instead, he was left behind by the race early on, and faced a 180km lone battle to get through the race's first Alpine stage inside the organisation-imposed time limit. And he did it.

'I'd finished when there was no reason to, when carrying on made no sense,' he wrote of the incident in his autobiography, *Racing Through The Dark*. 'I kept going when it would have been easier to give up.'

Against the odds, Millar finished that 2010 Tour, and would go on to finish the next three, too.

The 2014 Tour—again starting in England, as it had done seven years previously, when Millar had gone on the attack in front of his home crowd—should have been his 13th and final Tour. Here was a British rider ready to start on British soil, one of the most experienced riders on his Garmin-Sharp team, and in his last season as a pro. Yet he wasn't picked. His non-selection surprised him as much as anyone else; a dozen years of taking part—one for each year of his active career—only to be dropped in his final year. He was furious and even—with tongue firmly in cheek, surely—took to Twitter to ask whether anyone wanted to buy his bike: 'For sale. Been raced, not

much … Good condition. Reasonable offers please.'

It was quickly back off the market, however, and he was soon wishing his team-mates a good race before starting a summer job as a Tour pundit on British television.

But only two years earlier, Millar had roared—literally—across the line as winner of Stage 12. 'I am an ex-doper,' was his mantra to the flocks of journalists who surrounded Millar, utterly spent on the ground. The message was that if an ex-doper—most importantly, now a non-doper—could win a stage at the Tour, then it was a sign that the sport was cleaning itself up from the inside.

For better and for worse, Millar has played a large role in professional bike racing's doping story. Now footloose and fancy-free since retirement—albeit with a young family to look after—what will the next chapter in Millar's never-dull life bring?

PETER
KENNAUGH

THE 2014 BRITISH ROAD-RACE CHAMPION is desperate to make a return to the Tour de France, having ridden it, and finished it, just once when he helped his Team Sky leader Chris Froome to victory in 2013.

'I will never forget that moment,' he told the BBC of finishing on the Champs-Elysées, having helped his team-mate to win the world's biggest bike race. 'It will live with me forever.'

In fact, some would say that the diminutive climber possesses all the qualities necessary to one day win a race like the Tour himself. He just needs another chance or two at the Tour to really showcase them.

Kennaugh (pronounced 'Ken-yuk') had played a key role in the mountains for the yellow-clad Froome, regularly seen riding a high tempo on the front of the race to discourage rivals from jumping away up the road. He also proved his versatility as the kind of rider who's as comfortable piling on the pressure at the front of the bunch on the flat to set things up for the team's sprinter as he is climbing in the mountains, or even racing alone against the clock having been part of the gold-medal-winning British team pursuit team at the 2012 London Olympics.

So it was all-the-more mysterious that he wasn't again named on the nine-man roster sheet for 2014, and Kennaugh struggled to hide his frustration at his non-selection.

Instead, he went to the Tour of Austria, which takes place at the same time as the Tour de France, where he won the opening stage and held on to his lead for the rest of the race thanks to a virtuoso display of climbing during the

week-long event.

And those who followed his performances at the 2014 Commonwealth Games in Glasgow won't forget them in a hurry, either. First, Kennaugh scored a silver medal in the points race on the track, and then, a week later, he attacked almost from the gun at the road race to spend a long, lonely day at the head of affairs.

Like Mark Cavendish, Kennaugh hails from the Isle of Man, 90 miles north-west of Liverpool, in the middle of the Irish Sea. And Kennaugh represented the island in Glasgow, where the team was 'guest-managed' for the day by an off-duty Cavendish, recovering from the shoulder injury sustained in the

crash that forced him out of the Tour the previous month.

Cavendish would later describe Kennaugh's attack as 'a gutsy ride', although it was clear that it wasn't the move that had been discussed at the Isle of Man's pre-race team talk. It had been an almost impish desire to go on the attack on Kennaugh's part—and why not? It certainly entertained the roadside crowds and those watching at home on television on what was a miserably wet Glasgow day. At times, you even wondered whether Kennaugh could somehow stay the distance as you were willing him to. Alas, he was eventually reeled in with 50km of the 170km race to go, and it was Kennaugh's Sky team-mate Geraint Thomas, riding there

for Wales, who came good to take the victory, while Kennaugh somehow held on to finish eighth.

He was then picked for Sky's team for the Vuelta a España, which Froome, having crashed out of the Tour de France, was riding to win, and Kennaugh was part of the effort that carried their man to second overall behind Alberto Contador.

If Sky needed to see more from him before once again selecting him for their Tour team, it's exactly what Kennaugh went out and did in 2014.

It could prove to be that Sky are going to find him a difficult man to exclude from their Tour line-up from now on.

KENNAUGH ON STAGE 8 OF THE 2013 TOUR DE FRANCE

AND PACING CHRIS FROOME ON STAGE 15

STEVE
CUMMINGS

STEVE CUMMINGS STARTED OUT AS A TRACK-MAN, winning world-championship and Commonwealth titles, as well as an Olympic silver medal in the team pursuit, but had left the velodrome behind by the time the 2008 Beijing Olympics came around, where he rode both the road race and the time trial, both events at which he suffered due to the extreme heat.

Two years later, at the age of 29, Cummings made his debut at the 2010 Tour de France with the newly formed Team Sky, where he was charged with helping team leader Bradley Wiggins to try to improve on his fourth place overall of the year before. Cummings put his head down and got on with the job, finishing his first Tour in a very respectable 151st place, although Wiggins could only finish 24th in Paris, well off the pace, and a shadow of his 2009 self.

Cummings wasn't part of the squad for the 2011 Tour—where Wiggins's luck went from bad to worse, being forced to quit with a broken collar bone after just a week of racing. By the following year's race, which Wiggins of course dominated, Cummings had moved on to pastures new.

But his move away from Team Sky to the Swiss-American BMC squad for 2012 started badly when Cummings broke his pelvis in a crash at February's Tour of the Algarve in Portugal, only for him to recover from that and then break his wrist at the Tour of the Basque Country in April. And then in May he was forced out of the Tour of California after crash-landing on his injured wrist.

Cummings crashed a lot in the first half of 2012, and there were more spills to come. However, things seemed to be looking up when he was offered

TRAINING ON COBBLESTONES FOR THE 2010 TOUR

WITH FLECHA ON STAGE 14 IN 2010

the chance to start his second Tour that July, riding in the service of team leader and defending Tour champion Cadel Evans, although it was to be his former team leader, Wiggins, who would take Evans's crown. The Australian could only finish seventh, more than 15 minutes off the pace.

Cummings found himself on the deck again at that Tour, too, crashing heavily on Stage 17, but remounting to finish the stage, and the whole race, eventually placing 95th in Paris. He was in fact the only British rider

taking part in that year's race—along with Sky trio Wiggins, Chris Froome and Mark Cavendish, and Garmin's David Millar—not to win a stage.

But Cummings would end his 2012 season on a high at the Vuelta a España where he did win a stage—Stage 13 from Santiago de Compostela to Ferrol—after jumping away from a six-man breakaway group in the final 4km to win alone by four seconds from Orica-GreenEDGE's Cameron Meyer.

A fallow 2013 followed, but that gave way to 2014 when an injury-free

ON THE PROLOGUE OF THE 2012 TOUR

AFTER WINNING THE TIME TRIAL OF THE 2014 TOUR MÉDITERRANÉEN

start to the 2014 season saw Cummings in some of the best form of his career, which he put to devastating use to win both a stage and overall victory at that February's Tour of the Mediterranean.

A career spent mainly working for others has ensured Cummings has always been in demand; he possesses that rare gift of being happy to work for his team leaders for most of the season, while still having the ability to go for the win himself in certain situations.

In 2015, MTN-Qhubeka became his sixth team in a pro road career

that began in 2005 with the Belgian Landbouwkrediet-Colnago squad. He already has his two Tours de France under his belt, but when Cummings joined the South African set-up, he knew that his new team was a long way from being guaranteed a berth at the Tour.

That all changed at the start of the year when the African outfit was offered one of five 'wild-card' invitations, and Cummings will have as good a—if not considerably better—chance as anyone of being selected from a young, and sprinter-

heavy, stable.

The battle to earn one of just nine starting spots will be hard-fought— albeit in a friendly, team-matey kind of way—but just as Cummings was able to nab a stage at the 2012 Vuelta a España, attempting to do the same in France in July 2015, if the opportunity comes his way, won't be far from his mind.

SIMON
YATES

HE'S NO RELATION TO FORMER PRO SEAN YATES—who many will remember from the 1980s and 1990s, and for his stage win at the 1988 Tour de France in particular—but Simon Yates could well match, or even surpass, his compatriot's achievements at the Tour in the years to come.

Having been brought through to the top level by way of British Cycling's development programme, when Yates 'came of age' and was ready to turn pro for the 2014 season, he bucked the trend of accepting the advances of Team Sky—the natural path—to instead sign for Australian outfit Orica-GreenEDGE.

Eschewing Sky was an intentional move by Simon and his twin brother, Adam, in the hope of getting opportunities to ride for themselves, as opposed to in the service of others as may have been the case at the British team.

And the decision paid off handsomely when Orica threw the newly signed Yates brothers in at the deep end. Born in 1992—virtually the future—Simon and Adam quickly got up to speed in the professional peloton: in March's Paris–Nice, Simon finished with the lead group of 20 riders on the final stage, over a minute ahead of the chasers, before riding well at April's Tour of the Basque Country to finish 12th overall, while in early May, Adam picked up a stage win and took the overall honours at the Tour of Turkey.

As tends to happen with twins—and especially identical ones like the Yateses—Adam and Simon often get lumped together as one by the media, who struggle to pin down who's who, and who's won what. Their job was unfortunately made a lot easier at that Tour of Turkey when, while his brother was winning it, Simon was heading home after breaking his collar bone in a crash.

From there, their racing paths divulged somewhat for the rest of the season, and no one was more surprised than Simon when, having recovered from injury, he found himself named in the starting nine for the Tour, and on home soil in Britain, too.

With the non-selection for the 2014 race of the since-retired David Millar and the Movistar team's Alex Dowsett—another talented young British rider who is likely to make his Tour debut, if not in 2015, then in the next year or two—Simon Yates was one of only four Britons to start in Yorkshire. Given that the other three were defending Tour champion Chris Froome, sprint superstar Mark Cavendish and the well-established Geraint Thomas, Yates was in esteemed company.

And when Cavendish crashed out on the opening stage, Yates's star shone even brighter, and brighter still when the same fate befell Froome on Stage 5. Suddenly, it was just the affable Thomas and newbie Yates that the British press pursued, and Yates quickly got a taste of what he might have to deal with in future if his talent continues to grow.

When it was suggested to him by one reporter mid-way through the race that the team might pull him out early he replied with more than a

LEADING AN ESCAPE ON STAGE 14 OF THE 2014 TOUR

hint of indignation: 'Who said that!?'

Everyone except Yates, it seemed, was familiar with the practice of easing young, first-timers into the bubbling cauldron that is the Tour by not subjecting them to the full three weeks. Sure enough, at the conclusion of Stage 15, the announcement came that the team was sending Yates home.

'It was a once-in-a-lifetime opportunity, with the start in Yorkshire—almost home training roads, basically—and I think that's something I'll never really forget for the rest of my life,' Yates said on the team's website. 'It's been a great opportunity, and I'm looking forward to coming back.'

Despite his early Tour exit, his debut had been an impressive one, as Yates twice got into breakaways on hilly stages, giving a small glimpse of what the future might hold. He's going to be a rider to watch in the Alps and Pyrenees in the years to come.

LEANING IN ON STAGE 14 OF THE 2014 TOUR

Much of this book is devoted to riders who have done this or done that, paying homage to the greats, the legends, that have shaped the last five or ten years of professional cycling. And understandably so, but sport is constantly renewing and as one generation prepares its farewells, another is biting at their heels, ready to pick up from where they've left off. For cycling this could not be more true, with a prodigious group of young riders already making waves amongst the sport's biggest events. Five riders, Fabio Aru, Michael Kwiatkowski, Michael Matthews, Thibaut Pinot, and Nairo Quintana, have seemingly skipped a step, maybe ten, of their respective developments, and matured into world class riders at the tenderest of ages. Nairo Quintana has already won a Grand Tour, the Giro d'Italia. He very nearly won the Tour de France the year before. Thibaut Pinot, France's next great hope is a fabulous climber, but already enjoys a superstar status in his home country. Michael Kwiatkowski is a world champion, Fabio Aru, a scarily similar rider to Vincenzo Nibali, but six years his junior, and Michael Matthews may be the most versatile rider of the next decade. Between them, they'll have an immense impact on cycling's next decade, and it would be remiss not to do that justice.

YOUNG RIDERS

FABIO
ARU

MICHAL
KWIATKOWSKI

MICHAEL
MATTHEWS

THIBAUT
PINOT

NAIRO
QUINTANA

ALEX HINDS

FABIO
ARU

ITALY WAITED 16 LONG YEARS to dust off its Tour trophy cabinet through Sicilian Vincenzo Nibali. Nibali has steadily chipped away at the Grand Tour lark for the last five years, sweeping up a handful of podiums at the Giro d'Italia, Vuelta a España, and finally picked up the Tour de France in 2014. But, until recently Nibali was a lone force among a generation of Italians falling into anonymity. Ivan Basso is closing on retirement, Damiano Cunego looks lifeless, and the years of Simoni and Garzelli are long behind us. In Fabio Aru, however, Nibali's understudy at Astana, the country may have a rider to carry the torch in the next decade.

Aru hails from the small town of San Gavino Monreale, on the island of Sardinia. He found cycling relatively late, at the age of 15, having spent his younger years playing football and tennis. But when his family moved to the mountain-set town of Villacidro, Aru's interest in the two-wheeled sport was sparked. With the help of his parents he saved to buy a race bike, and in his late teens he was showing good promise on the Italian amateur scene.

As a junior he took initially to cyclo-cross and mountain biking. He raced the World Cup circuit and the World Championships. He wasn't all that bad at 'cross and might well have gone far in the discipline had he given it a year or two in the senior ranks. But instead in 2009, as an 18-year-old, he was recruited to ride the road for the highly regarded Palazzago amateur team, under the wing of legendary directeur Olivano Locatelli.

His initial progress wasn't spectacular, his nerves and unfamiliarity with bunch riding often scuppered his chances to perform. He did distinguish

FROOME AND ARU IN THE 2014 VUELTA A ESPANA

ARU WINNING STAGE 18 OF THE VUELTA A ESPANA

himself early as a natural climber but lacked results to show for it. By 2010 he was finding his confidence, however, and results started to present themselves. He was fourth at the Giro Ciclistico della Valle d'Aosta, a short, mountainous stage race for espoirs (under 23), and just outside the top ten in the 'Baby' Giro d'Italia.

Holding the Italian back from further progression was his impulsiveness. He'd often launch himself early and hope to hold on, only to find himself faltering in the last 10 to 20 kilometres. He learnt from his mistakes in 2011, putting together a far more mature all-round

season. He won Valle d'Aosta, and was fourth at the 'Baby' Giro.

Halfway through the 2012 season Aru was signed to the Astana team on a trainee contract, with a professional ride with the team for the two years after. His neo-pro year saw him play a major role in Vincenzo Nibali's maiden Giro d'Italia victory. Aru was frequently by Nibali's side in the mountains, and though he was largely under the radar, he did post a respectable 42nd overall, and importantly stayed with the team through until the finish in Brescia.

With only one Grand Tour under his belt, Aru was impressing his directeur Giuseppe Martinelli

QUINTANA WITH ARU AND URAN ON STAGE 21 OF THE 2014 GIRO D'ITALIA

enough to be thrown into the deep end in 2014, assuming a co-leadership role for the 97th Giro d'Italia. While former Giro champion Michele Scarponi was the nominal number one, Aru outshone his more accomplished team-mate, riding to maiden stage win on the Montecampione, and finishing third overall. He rode an equally impressive Vuelta a España later in the year, where he finished fifth overall, and edged Chris Froome on the mountain summit of Monte Castrove, to take a second Grand Tour stage of the year.

Aru is still a little hot-headed, an attribute he'll perhaps naturally shed as he gets older, but at present it's clearly holding him back. And his time trial desperately needs work. Unlike Nibali, who's an ace against the clock, Aru is suspect, and while that's fine for a rider that can devastate his rivals in the high mountains, it is something that will prevent him from stepping from the Grand Tour podium to the top-step.

Aru will ride the 2015 season with the Astana team, and is expected to make the Giro d'Italia his immediate focus over the next few seasons. Expect to see Aru challenging at the Tour in 2017 and beyond.

MICHAL
KWIATKOWSKI

MICHAL KWIATKOWSKI IS AMONG THE MOST ENIGMATIC riders in today's professional peloton. Much of that comes down to his youth; he's still discovering what kind of rider he is, where he excels, where he doesn't. He's discovering the kind of person he is too. His head is often in the clouds, he'll be joking around with team-mates and journalists before a Tour stage, laughing and carrying on, when others are quietly going about their pre-race routines. He's a kid at heart and his tiny frame and bare face make him look like one too.

But once the Pole gets on the bike his playful personality manifests in a menacing style of racing. Kwiatkowski is instinctively unpredictable, at home as much attacking from afar as he is waiting in the peloton for a sprint finish. It helps that his talents run deep; he's ridden high up in the general classification at the Tour de France, poked his head up in the Ardennes, he can ride cobbles, he can even sprint. Versatile, stubbornly strong, and unpredictable—basically the worst nightmare of any rider who has the misfortune of coming across him.

Not that this is news for those that have followed Kwiatkowski's career from the juniors. 'Kwia' was the kind of child prodigy that's known nothing but success from a young age, cleaning up all over Europe, enjoying a near invincible run as he collected junior European and World titles for fun. So good was the young Pole, that he essentially skipped the customary apprenticeship of aspiring professionals in the espoirs ranks (under 23), and opted instead to sign his first professional contract with Spanish team Caja Rural at the age of 19.

KWIATKOWSKI IN THE WHITE JERSEY, WITH SAGAN IN GREEN AND NIBALI IN THE OVERALL LEADER'S YELLOW JERSEY

GAVAZZI, KWIATKOWSKI AND HAGEN ON THE PODIUM AFTER THE 2014 TROFEO DEIA

IN THE WHITE JERSEY ON STAGE 5 IN 2013

A year in the continental ranks was enough, and Kwiatkowski was signed into the WorldTour before his 21st birthday, signing with RadioShack in 2011, and Quick Step in 2012, where he's stayed ever since. Kwiatkowski's versatility has left managers scratching their heads as to how to best utilise the prodigious Pole. His featherweight physique makes him a natural climber, but because he can also punch out short bursts of power to attack or distance his rivals, he's an obvious candidate for success in the hilly classics.

However with such an emphasis on the Tour in the cycling calendar it was little surprise that Kwiatkowski was trialled as a Tour rider in 2013. He performed admirably, pipped out of the top ten by Thibaut Pinot, but still finishing a respectable 11th overall. At 23 it was a promising result, but it was decidedly mediocre in the context of what's come from him since.

The last 12 months has seen Kwiatkowski remove himself from the Grand Tour pool and focus instead on one-week stage races, and single day events, where he's always excelled. The move has been a godsend to Kwiatkowski's career, shedding the expectation and physical toll associated with three week riding, and giving him more ammunition, and more exuberance to flourish in selected events on the calendar.

Notable was Kwiatkowski's form in the Ardennes, where he was unlucky to come up against two older, far more experienced rivals in Simon Gerrans and Alejandro Valverde, but still found himself consistently competitive. The older pair have near three decades of experience between them, hundreds of thousands of kilometres in their legs, and the kind of hardened resolve it takes to win. Yet they looked only fractionally superior to Kwiatkowksi

in La Fleche Wallone and Liège –Bastogne–Liège, where the Pole collected two third placings.

He got the better of them, however, later in the year when he won the World Championship road race in Ponferrada, Spain, escaping solo after catching his rivals napping on the descent before the final climb and then holding off the chase to win the rainbow stripes.

His rapid ascendancy in one-day races is a sign of what we can come to expect from the young Pole, who will be a tough rider to beat in any one-day race he puts his mind to targeting as he matures. It'll make him a viable stage hunter at the Tour de France, too, but whether he can go further, and one day compete for yellow, might rely more on his will, than any physical limitation.

Michal Kwiatkowski will ride the 2015 season with the Etixx-Quick Step team.

MICHAEL
MATTHEWS

IT'S DEEPLY APPROPRIATE THAT MICHAEL MATTHEWS bases himself in
Monaco when he's not in Australia; a city of fast cars, beautiful people, and
exorbitant wealth. Matthews has taken a liking to its expensive charms. He has
an expansive luxury apartment in one of the city's most exclusive buildings, he
drives a Porsche, and treats himself with all sorts of golden trinkets. It's what
has given Matthews his nickname, 'Bling'. But it would do him a disservice
to colour, or to confuse, Matthews' high-life tastes as signs of recklessness, or
even weakness, in his character as an athlete. The Australian for one, doesn't
drink, and sees his luxuries as hard-earned material rewards for the amount of
work he puts in, day in, day out as an athlete.

And he is a phenomenal athlete, and one that more importantly, works
damn hard for it. Matthews was identified in his teens as a potential talent
by the Australian Capital Territory Academy of Sport, after a school teacher
noted his natural aerobic ability. Matthews then linked up with the Australian
Institute of Sport, and became an instant hit with his breakneck-sprint.
Unlike a number of his compatriots, however, Matthews could climb too, and
he wasn't bad at holding long threshold efforts ideal for efforts against the
clock. That combination of speed and endurance talent in cycling is rare, but
Matthews is blessed with both, and it wasn't long before he was showing them
to the world.

At age 19, he was riding for Rabobank's development squad, leaving the
comfort of family and home to travel the world. He was also quick to the
winner's circle, taking victories in Malaysia at the Tour de Langkawi where he

MATTHEWS WINS STAGE 3 OF THE 2014 VUELTA A ESPANA

faced far-senior professionals, and racked up strong overall results in Europe. He, remembering he's a sprinter here, placed eighth overall at the Tour de l'Avenir, the race widely considered to be a gauge on future Tour de France yellow jersey contenders, and capped his season splendidly with the under-23 world title. All at the age of 19. He turned WorldTour with Rabobank the following season.

What's scary about Matthews is what he's done since. He's clocked stage wins at the Giro d'Italia and

Vuelta a España, he's worn the leader's jersey too, at both, and his resilience, in the same vein as Simon Gerrans, has made him a stronger proposition in the Ardennes and races like the Tour of Flanders. Matthews has worked hard to hone his climbing, and in the last few years has moved from a fairweather sprinter to one that can win atop small bergs, or cols. At the Giro, case in point, he edged a group containing Cadel Evans to take his first individual stage in Montecassino.

He's also thrown off one of his former shackles—his nerve. In his first two years Matthews was often caught erring on the side of caution in big bunch finishes, where the high speeds and heightened danger of crashes are at their peak. At Rabobank Matthews was often cradled by elder compatriot Graeme Brown, who helped guide the younger sprinter to his finishing quarry through his own experience. Without Brown, Matthews could struggle, but he has thrown off his fears of late, finding no trouble

AND STAGE 6 OF THE GIRO D'ITALIA THE SAME YEAR

navigating Grand Tour bunches with the best of them.

Another former professional, Baden Cooke, has helped Matthews believe in himself more. Cooke has worked to encourage Matthews to look at races like Flanders, the World Championships or stages at the biggest Grand Tours, and see them as achievable targets. It's apparently working, with Matthews finding a firmer footing in the top tier under Cooke's tutelage.

If Matthews is on his game he'll win classics, stages, world championships by a league, he's freakishly talented, he's that good. He has few natural rivals, and if he can further work and build on his consistency it's hard to envisage him not going on to collect a Cavendish-esque haul of trophies in his professional cycling career.

Matthews currently rides in the WorldTour with Orica-GreenEDGE. He's expected to focus increasingly on the Tour de France in the next few seasons, and with his versatility, is a logical challenger for the sprinter's green jersey.

THIBAUT
PINOT

IT'S BEEN NEAR ON 30 YEARS SINCE a Frenchman last won a Tour de France, and with every passing year that sorry streak continues, the national anxiety to anoint a new potential winner grows. It's burdened some of the country's most promising young talents with unnecessary pressure, and distracted others with the allures of superstardom, even before they've properly fulfilled their potentials.

But after a number of false starts, Sandy Casar, Sylvain Chavanel, and going back further, Richard Virenque—who despite a decorated career, never quite won the Tour—France now has one, two, perhaps even three viable hopes they can pin their fortunes too. The gaunt, but fluid climber Pierre Rolland is one. The fresh faced Romain Bardet is another. But the most serious challenger among France's youth is Thibaut Pinot.

Pinot sprung to the attention of Tour fans in 2012 when he briefly wore the Tour's white jersey, as best young rider, and finished 10th overall. But what truly piqued their interest was his stage victory in Porrentruy. On a stage that proved harder than it appeared on paper, Pinot showed class, to sneak away from the bunch and claw back, then pass, Swede Frederik Kessiakoff on the final climb of the day—Col de la Croix. Pinot held his advantage to the finish, and was a very popular winner.

The French love riders who ride with panache. Emotional, fighting riding makes the French proud. If they can win, too, well that's a bonus. Thomas Voeckler, perhaps exemplifies that sort of mentality. But Voeckler's physical limitations mean he will never win the Tour de France. Not so of Pinot, who

marshalls both popular support as one of France's new darlings but rises above distraction; a steady head on his shoulders, keeping himself focused throughout a three week Grand Tour, and blessed too with the physical talent to match it with the best. Pinot became the youngest rider to finish in the Tour's top ten in 2012 in Tour's modern era, not by chance.

Pinot's performance led French newspaper *L'Equipe* to name the young rider, dangerously, the next Bernard Hinault. Hinault himself called the young prodigy a rider France hadn't seen in a generation, and praised his racing mind. But, weary of riders like Chavanel, who'd stalled in their development after promising starts, he also was quick to play down the media's overhyping of Pinot who he warned could fall as quickly as he'd risen.

That caution proved sage when Pinot struggled to overcome a phobia of descending at speed at the 2013 Tour de France. It was a debilitating setback for a rider whose greatest strength, was ability to climb in the high mountains. But what goes up, must come down, and where the

LEADING NIBALI ON STAGE 16 OF THE 2014 TOUR

PINOT IN ACTION EARLIER DURING STAGE 10

race didn't end on a mountaintop, but on the valley floor, Pinot found himself losing minutes as his nerve got the better of him. It threatened to derail his career, but Pinot did turn it around in the months after July, and made a strong return to form, with lessened pressure at the Vuelta a España where he was seventh.

The Frenchman would show himself to be the real deal in 2014, riding himself onto the Tour de France's final podium, behind Jean Christophe-Peraud and winner Vincenzo Nibali, in a ride that confirmed his abundant talent. While Pinot was no match for Nibali in the high mountains, he did outperform BMC's Tejay van Garderen, a likely future rival, and veteran Spaniard Alejandro Valverde. Impressively too for a rider that had been criticised for his suspect time trial, a key weakness in his Grand Tour credentials, he rode a strong penultimate day chrono effort to Perigueux to seal his place on the podium.

Pinot needs only to make marginal improvements in the next few seasons to edge himself from the podium of a Grand Tour, to the top of the dais. He has a healthy appetite to attack in the mountains, and liberal self belief; if he keeps himself fit and his attention on Grand Tour success there's really nothing stopping him from ending France's Tour drought.

Pinot has a contract with team FDJ until the end of the 2016 season. He's expected to make the Tour de France his major objective in the foreseeable future.

MAJKA, PINOT, NIBALI AND SAGAN SHORTLY AFTER THE START OF THE FINAL STAGE OF THE 2014 TOUR

NAIRO
QUINTANA

THE BIGGEST QUESTION OVER NAIRO QUINTANA is not what he can do, but what he can't. The poker-faced youngster has already eclipsed the achievements of any Colombian that's come before him. And he's yet, one can only think at 25, to really hit his stride.

After winning the Giro d'Italia in 2014, he is now one of cycling's most recognisable names, but it's a long way from Quintana's humble beginnings. The Colombian hails from a small settlement outside the town of Combita in the country's mountainous heart, and was first introduced to the bike as a means to get to school. Quintana had previously had to walk a 32km return journey to get to school and back, and was getting exhausted doing it on a regular basis. A believer in his education, his father saved up to purchase young Nairo a bike, and it wasn't long before Quintana was making short work not just of the daily commute but of longer, harder rides in the surrounding country.

He didn't dream of becoming a professional but he did race from a young age, and with a lean physique, and an enviable cardio system, he proved to be very good. His father, who remains one of his biggest supporters, often lacked money for Quintana's race entry fees, but would negotiate with race organisers to allow Nairo to race free, and pay back the entry fee from what he'd won. It was a bold strategy, but Quintana was such a talent, that the deal worked out more often than not. Quintana did eventually earn himself his first amateur contract in 2009, at 19, with a locally-backed team in his home region, Boyacá Es Para Vivirla, where he honed his craft further.

WINNING STAGE 20 OF THE 2013 TOUR

In 2010, Quintana became the first Colombian to win the prestigious Tour de l'Avenir off the back of a strong showing in the French Alps. That victory garnered him huge attention, and no shortage of offers from bigger teams, but Quintana chose to remain out of the WorldTour in 2011 in the interests of developing himself better in the sport's second tier. That decision proved to be a wise one, as when he did step up, with Movistar in 2012, he was quickly winning against seasoned professionals. Quintana clinched the first stage race win of his professional career at the Vuelta a Murcia, and followed that later in the year when he won the Route du Sud.

Quintana has blown those results out of the water in the last couple of years. Rarely do riders so young flourish on the biggest stages, Grand Tours, but in consecutive years Quintana has not just participated, but imprinted himself on the professional cycling scene. Even

playing second fiddle to Alejandro Valverde at Movistar, Quintana distinguished himself in his debut at the Tour de France in 2014. Many of the sport's biggest names, including Contador, Chris Froome and Joaquim Rodriguez, could only watch as Quintana shrugged off the ripping grades of legendary climbs like Alpe d'Huez and Mont Ventoux, and ploughed away time and time again. Froome fortunately was in prime position in yellow after distancing Quintana in the race's opening stanza, but as the Tour approached Paris, the Colombian was getting stronger and stronger. By the race's penultimate stage, on Annecy–Semnoz, Quintana had Froome on the ropes, but had run out of road to catch him. He finished second overall, and took the home the best climber's prize, the polka dot jersey.

To string together three weeks of largely consistent riding, faltering only slightly when his exuberance got the better of him early in the Alps,

was impressive. His improvement over the three week journey, unusual for a rider of his age, a quality that will put him in excellent stead to be a force in Grand Tours for years to come. In many ways of course, he is already. Last year Quintana triumphed at the Giro d'Italia with a mature, and determined three week performance, becoming the first Colombian to win the Italian Grand Tour. Unlike his breakout ride at the Tour, Quintana was no longer an unknown quantity and had added pressure to deal with, and yet, after a turbulent start, fought out his way into the lead by the race's second week, and looked untouchable thereafter.

The final frontier for Quintana remains a Tour win, but on his record so far, it's really not a question of if, but when. Quintana, 25, currently rides for Movistar, and has a contract with the team until 2017. He's expected to target the Tour de France in 2015 and 2016.

ATTACKING EARLIER ON STAGE 20 OF THE 2013 TOUR

AND EARLIER ON THE TOUR, SPEEDING ON STAGE 11

Despite sitting more than 10,000km from Europe, Australia and Australians have a rich association with the Tour de France that dates back to 1914. The country's first two participants, Don Kirkham and Iddo 'Snowy' Munro, performed admirably, each settling inside the top twenty in what set an immediate high bar. Others followed in the wake with mixed success. Sir Hubert Opperman, in an Australasian team, ran 12th in 1932, but even by the time Phil Anderson bettered that result some 50 years later, riders from the island-continent were rare novelties to an event that had a distinctly European flavour. Belgians and French, Italians and Spaniards; cycling was a small sport held together by the passion and history of a handful of countries. With the arrival of American Tour winner in Greg Lemond in 1986, the proliferation of better broadcast infrastructure, and a change in the Tour's management, the race developed an international appeal, and with that came riders from all over the world. A trickle, and then a legion of Australians were among them, fighting to ply their trade in the European peloton.

By the 1990s Australians were flooding the professional scene, and doing well, and by the early 2000s riders from down under were not just commonplace, but performing with remarkable success. Robbie McEwen was the first to win a major jersey at the Tour de France in 2002, when he won the *maillot vert*, and that opened the floodgates to ever-greater success in the decade since. Australians have now won four green sprinter's jerseys, a glut of stage wins, and in 2011, the country picked up its first Tour de France victory through Cadel Evans. They form integral parts of the world's biggest teams, and below, are five of the current crop's best.

THE AUSTRALIANS

MARK
RENSHAW

MICHAEL
ROGERS

SIMON
GERRANS

MATT
GOSS

RICHIE
PORTE

ALEX HINDS

MARK
RENSHAW

HE MAY NOT WIN AS OFTEN AS SOME of the other Australians on this list, but Mark Renshaw's ability to elevate those around him makes him an invaluable part of any team, and impossible to overlook.

Long-time friend Mark Cavendish is one of the fastest men on two wheels, but he would have been far less prolific in the last five years had it not been for the work of Renshaw. The Australian has made a trade of acting leadout man, a role he's performed in the service of some of cycling's biggest names: Tom Boonen, Thor Hushovd, Theo Bos, and perhaps most famously, Cavendish.

So successful was Cavendish under Renshaw, that the partnership had an aura of invincibility about it. If Cavendish was delivered to the 200 metre mark without touching the front, as he so often was by the Australian, there could be no other winner. Between 2009 and 2011, the best years of their partnership, Cavendish collected 15 Tour de France stages, and in 2011, the green sprinter's jersey.

Lead-outs appear easy when executed perfectly, a seamless transition of power and speed from one rider in a line to the next, with the final in the line—the team's designated sprinter—flung forth with little to do. When they're pulled off correctly, they're smooth, beautiful exhibitions of discipline and communication; a team time trial of sorts, but one among the chaos of peloton of a hundred other riders, fighting for the finish themselves.

With only Cavendish, Bos or Hushovd behind him, Renshaw calls the shots in this hectic, frantic finale. In a cool, calm collected manner, that few can

CAVENDISH WITH RENSHAW ON STAGE 20

muster in such a tense environment, he barks orders to his team-mates in front to ramp the pace up, back off, or reposition; all while travelling at upwards of 60 to 70km/h. These are split-second decisions, and they require mutual trust among every man involved. A wrong decision, or a momentary pause, can be the difference between a stage win and being locked out—even a race-ending crash.

What makes Renshaw so good is his consistency in reading this chaos and seeing a clear path. Additionally, his ability to accelerate keeps all but the best sprinters in the world struggling to keep pace. In 2011, so violent was his acceleration in the last few hundred metres of the Tour de France's final stage on the Champs-Elysées, Cavendish glued to his wheel, needn't have sprinted.

He has erred of course, he's

only human. In 2010, on the Tour de France's Stage 11 to Bourg-les-Valence, he overplayed his hand if only slightly in tussling with New Zealander Julian Dean. Dean, marginally, had stolen a march on Renshaw, leaving the Australian, and his team-mate Cavendish, behind in a bind. But instead of ceding the road to Dean, Renshaw thread the needle with a daring balancing act to keep himself and Cavendish in the hunt. Riding shoulder to shoulder with Dean, Renshaw kept himself from the barriers to his left by headbutting Dean to make room. It wasn't pretty but it got the job done; Cavendish collecting the stage honours comfortably. But Renshaw was booted from the race for unsportsmanlike behaviour, a charge he, to this day, contests.

It is, however, an aberration in a career marked by selflessness and

professionalism. In a sport that's defined by team-work but that celebrates the individual, Renshaw has been notably selfless. Perhaps in the decades to come, his name will fade from memory, but in those of the careers he's helped succeed, there'll be an eternal debt of gratitude.

Renshaw, 33 in October, has lost some of his sharpness in recent years, and even as he's resumed his partnership with Cavendish at a new team, Omega Pharma–Quick Step, the sheen of invulnerability the two once had is now lacking its former lustre. That said, Renshaw remains a formidable force in the professional peloton, and a welcome asset for any sprinter that's fortunate enough to have him leading them out.

Renshaw will ride the 2015 season with the Etixx-Quick Step team.

WITH CAVENDISH AND HINCAPIE ON STAGE 21 OF THE 2009 TOUR

ON STAGE 12 OF THE 2014 TOUR

JUBILANT WITH TEAMMATE CAVENDISH ON THE FINISH LINE AT THE 2009 TOUR

MICHAEL
ROGERS

WHILE MICHAEL ROGERS HAS HAD HIS SHARE of individual successes; a three-time time trial world champion, a winner of stages at the Tour de France and Giro d'Italia, his biggest contribution to teams has always been the way he's masterminded others' accomplishments. Rogers has a brain hardwired for bike racing, a tactical nous that has made him invaluable as a captain on the road to any team that's been able to meet his hefty price tag.

Like Renshaw, Rogers' physical attributes aren't bad, they're just not world-beating, but his ability to read a race situation, and make the right calls, time and time again makes him a sought after asset for the world's best riders and teams. Rogers has worked as a lieutenant for Grand Tour winners Bradley Wiggins, Chris Froome and Alberto Contador, and has been integral to the success of teams like T-Mobile, Team Sky and Tinkoff-Saxo.

Rogers background is in time trialling, which explains his pedantic, scientific approach to his cycling. Rogers is a tinkerer, always reviewing and overhauling his bike, his training, and his diet in a bid to get peak performance out of himself—and the same applies to the teams he's worked with. For the early years of his career it was thought that Rogers would go on to develop himself as a Grand Tour contender, after a promising start winning a handful of smaller stage races in Europe in the early 2000s. But after serving an apprenticeship under Richard Virenque at Quick Step, and then Jan Ullrich at T-Mobile, his career stalled, never quite fulfilling the promise his younger talent suggested.

His highest finish at the Tour de France came in 2006 when he finished

ninth overall as a de facto for T-Mobile co-leader after Jan Ullrich was forced to withdraw due to his association with the Spanish doping sting, Operacion Puerto. A crash on the descent of the treacherous Cormet de Roseland the following year, that left him with a broken collarbone, denied Rogers his chance to better that result in 2007, and a recurring battle with mononucleosis made the 2008 and 2009 seasons difficult ones.

With his health weighing him down, Rogers toned down his own ambitions, and stepped into the role of super-domestique at Team Sky. The decision didn't immediately pay dividends, but by 2011, Rogers was helping steer the British team to world domination. His final year with the team saw Rogers architect a Tour de France win for Bradley Wiggins, before departing Team Sky for Tinkoff-Saxo, in 2012.

So precise and steady-handed was Rogers leadership at Team Sky, that he was known to make tactical calls on the road based on the number of watts he was currently putting out; calculating what the riders around him would need to be producing themselves to keep up, and helping that guide his decision to push the tempo higher or sit back. On the stage to the Col du Tourmalet Rogers told his Team Sky team-mates to allow Vincenzo Nibali and Jurgen van den Broeck to escape, knowing with the power he was currently putting out, maintaining their gap to the finish would require a super-human effort. They were, as he predicted, brought back into the fold before the summit.

CHASING ON STAGE 8 OF THE 2014 TOUR

The last two years of Michael Rogers' career have seen him truly flourish, finding himself more relaxed, and more at home perhaps than ever at Tinkoff. Rogers' 2014, particularly, with the exception of some time on the sidelines due to a now overturned suspension for clenbuterol, was a standout. Rogers won the first Grand Tour stages of his career at the ripe old age of 35, taking a pair of golden opportunities to win solo at the Giro and backing up later at the Tour de France with an emotional victory in the Pyreneean town of Bagnerres de Luchon.

Rogers, 36 in December, is approaching the twilight of his career, but evidenced by 2014, he's hardly slowing down. Don't expect Rogers to go anywhere in the next few years, this is a rider who's unlikely to rest until he's delivered Alberto Contador to another Tour de France victory.

Rogers will ride the 2015 Tour de France with Tinkoff-Saxo.

ON STAGE 7 OF THE 2012 TOUR

LEADING AN ATTACK ON STAGE 13 OF THE 2013 TOUR

SIMON
GERRANS

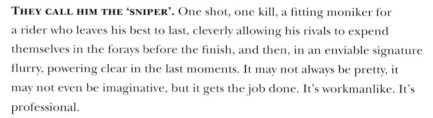

THEY CALL HIM THE 'SNIPER'. One shot, one kill, a fitting moniker for a rider who leaves his best to last, cleverly allowing his rivals to expend themselves in the forays before the finish, and then, in an enviable signature flurry, powering clear in the last moments. It may not always be pretty, it may not even be imaginative, but it gets the job done. It's workmanlike. It's professional.

And professional is Simon Gerrans to a tee. A rider who may not have been gifted the natural athletic talent of some of his rivals, but who has worked hard throughout his career to polish and refine every aspect of his body, mind and will—to sculpt himself as, now, a rider that's been successful wherever he's aimed.

Each of his growing list of victories is borne out of a precise, calculated approach, that leaves little to chance. Every box ticked, every possible avenue explored, to maximise his race day potential. Matched with a patient, intelligent style to his racing, Gerrans rightly has a reputation as one of the most feared one-day riders of his generation.

His record speaks for itself. He's taken scalps at the Tour de France, Vuelta a España and Giro d'Italia. In 2012, in the Italian Monument, Milan-San Remo, he ousted classic king Fabian Cancellara and Giro d'Italia and Tour de France champion Vincenzo Nibali, no less, in a three-up sprint. He's worn the yellow jersey at the Tour, he's won three Tours Down Under, two national championships, and last year, capped things off spectacularly at the biggest and oldest one day race on the professional calendar, Liège–Bastogne–Liège.

ON STAGE 3 OF THE 2013 TOUR

In doing so, he became the first Antipodean in the race's history to win the storied classic, and sealed his status as one of the all-time greats.

In Australia, his success has made him a poster boy of the sport. His broad smile, boyish face—is he really 30-something?—and selfless attitude around fans and the media make him instantly likable, and easy to deal with. It's Gerrans who's last to leave an autograph session with fans, and the first to put his hand up for another. He doesn't revel in the spotlight, but he understands his duty as a successful athlete and is a keen ambassador for its growth and future prosperity.

Interestingly, his status now among the world's best is starkly contrasted to his inauspicious beginnings in the tiny Victorian town of Mansfield, where he grew up.

There, west of the Mount Buller ski slopes, and a short drive from Bright, one of Australia's most renowned mountain bike parks, Gerrans made his start with the sport as a way of rehabilitating a knee-injury he'd sustained motorcycling.

The long, lonely roads, deserted in summer as the ski resorts shut down, with plenty of climbing, and no shortage of variety were fruitful ground for Gerrans to discover the sport's charm, but it took many years for ideas of grandeur to evolve from anything but fantasy. A family friend, Tour de France cyclist Phil Anderson, who would become a mentor to Gerrans, initially believed the young Australian to be unlikely to go far in the sport, although he helped him in any way he could. Veteran coach Dave Sanders too, who worked with Gerrans at the Victorian

and Australian Institutes of Sport, was pleasantly surprised to see the Australian break through, and then flourish in the professional ranks. And flourish he did.

Gerrans has ridden in the top tier of cycling for five different teams, AG2R Prévoyance, where he got his first break, the Credit Agricole, where he first won a Tour de France stage, Cervelo, where he had a career purple patch, and Team Sky, before finally landing at Australian team Orica-GreenEDGE, which he joined at the start of 2012 as a founding member.

Gerrans, 35 in May, signed a new three-year deal with Orica-GreenEDGE in 2014, that's expected to take him to the end of his career.

PUMPING IT ON STAGE 11 OF THE 2011 TOUR

ON STAGE 1 OF THE 2012 TOUR

WINNING STAGE 3 OF THE 2013 TOUR

MATT
GOSS

IT'S SAID CONFIDENCE BREEDS SUCCESS and in Matt Goss's case it's a maxim that could not be more apt. Goss is the kind of rider that looks unbeatable when he's on form, peerless in his speed and acceleration, but becomes near anonymous when he's not. Hot, and cold. He's enjoyed considerable success in some seasons, besting Mark Cavendish and Peter Sagan in sprints, Fabian Cancellera in the classics, and rubbed shoulders with the world's best as an equal. But he's been a lost force these last three years, drifting in his career after joining Orica-GreenEDGE, seemingly unable to replicate his former dominance. Now at MTN-Qhubeka Goss has eased himself of the burdens of leadership, slotting into a team where he hopes to rediscover his former talent.

Goss began his career like so many Australians, on the velodrome. He was a star of the junior track squad and, after turning 18, was part of the Australian Institute of Sport's hybrid squad of track and road riders based in Italy, where he thrived. He was a world champion on the track in Bordeaux, 2006 at the age of 19, riding a blistering time in the team pursuit with Peter Dawson, Stephen Wooldridge and Mark Jamieson to beat the Brits and enjoyed a prolific year in the European amateur road scene. It was enough to put himself firmly in the shop window for prospective teams. He had several offers but opted to sign for CSC at the close of 2006, joining compatriot Stuart O'Grady in what was then one of the world's biggest teams.

He was untroubled living in Europe, comfortably adapting to the time away from home as if he'd been a seasoned pro. Before his 23rd birthday he

had a string of results in the classics, including podiums in Kuurne-Brussel-Kuurne and Gent-Wevelgem a win in Paris-Bruxelles, and a growing a collection of stage wins at smaller races. Goss was earning a reputation as a hard-man with a powerful kick. The kind of rider his rivals were reluctant to get to the finish with, and his attitude, that tooth and nail desire to get over the line first, bred growing respect.

The Australian's career upped a gear in 2010 when he joined HTC-Columbia. Under the tutelage of team director Allan Peiper, Goss honed his top-end speed, and became an increasing threat in bunch sprints. At the Giro d'Italia he scored his first Grand Tour stage win, almost accidentally after distancing team sprinter Andre Greipel in a chaotic finish in Campania. And while he took a backseat at the Tour to Mark Cavendish, Goss was growing into a formidable sprinter. That reputation ballooned the following year when he added a handful of wins at the Tour Down Under, Paris-Nice, and the Tour of Oman before taking the biggest win of his career at the Italian Classic, Milan-San Remo. Goss had both the grit to get himself in the leading group over the Poggio with some hand climbers, and then the smarts to cover himself off the descent in the run to the finish to keep things together for a sprint.

In September, he capped his year with a narrow silver medal at the UCI Road World Championships in Copenhagen, with only Cavendish, who edged the Australian by a whisker, keeping Goss out of the rainbow jersey.

But rather than accelerate off this momentum in 2012, Goss's career stalled. Goss's 2011 earned him a bumper contract with Orica-GreenEDGE, and a leadership role, but the Australian withered in the limelight. Partially this was a function of the pressure placed on him, but partly too, was the push from Orica for Goss to become a dedicated sprinter. While he'd become more of a pure sprinter at HTC, Goss was far

GIVING IT HIS ALL ON STAGE 12 OF THE 2012 TOUR

from the kind of rider that benefited from the kind of disciplined lead-out train that Orica was trying to build. Unsurprisingly, and despite Goss's best efforts, the partnership failed to prosper. Despite finishing in the top four on six stage of the 2012 Tour, it perpetually felt as if Goss was the square peg in the round hole.

That conspired to see Goss's career trajectory take a dive, and as Orica looked elsewhere for its success as Gerrans took on increasing responsibility, Goss fell further from his best. Leaving the team as he did by mutual consent at the close of 2014 could be the kind of change Goss needs to reinvigorate his career. He remains, along with Simon

Gerrans, the only Australian to win a monument, and should he return to his former best his sprint should make him competitive in the more selective bunch dashes once more at the Tour. More than anything Goss needs to play to his strengths. He was never the same kind Mark Cavendish or Marcel Kittel and never will be. If Goss can remember this, and be steered in that direction by his teams, he'll be winning more, be happier with what he's doing, and ultimately be more successful.

Goss will ride the 2015 season with the MTN-Qhubeka team, and is expected to target the classics and Tour stages in the next few years.

RICHIE
PORTE

THE RETIREMENT OF CADEL EVANS, in February 2015, has left a huge gulf in Australian cycling, but if anyone can build on what Evans has done in Grand Tours, it has to be Richie Porte. Porte is a very different rider to Evans, both in style and physique, but he does have the gifts to compete at the peak of the sport in Grand Tours. Whether he's given the freedom to unleash them at Team Sky is another question entirely.

Born in Launceston, Tasmania, Porte's start in cycling came after a brief career in triathlon. A naturally gifted swimmer and cyclist, Porte would often find himself leading triathlons early, only to see himself mown down by better runners on the final leg. But, his strength on the bike made a Tasmanian cycling coach, Andrew Christie-Johnston, take notice. Porte, tired of a frustrating experience in Tri, accepted Christie-Johnston's offer to spend more time in cycling through his amateur team, Praties. The partnership was a hit, and after a year learning the ins and outs of bunch riding, Porte dominated the domestic scene in Australia, and was quickly snapped up to ride the WorldTour.

After five short years in the professional peloton Porte has now established himself as one of the strongest stage racers around, and as he enters his 30s he has both the physical and mental maturity to set out to win a Grand Tour, fortune willing. In his favour is the team around him, led by one of the sport's most renowned coaches, compatriot Tim Kerrison. Kerrison has helped former Tour winners Bradley Wiggins and Chris Froome reach their winning potential at the British super-squad Team Sky, and he's been working closely with Porte since 2012 to achieve the same thing.

The results have already been encouraging: in 2013 Porte became the first Australian to win the prestigious season-opener Paris–Nice, considered a truncated version of the Tour de France, and has served as an able apprentice to Wiggins and Froome on their way to their respective Tour victories. One of the key images of the 2013 Tour de France, and critical to delivering Froome to the final yellow jersey, was Porte's performance on the Alpe d'Huez, where, as the Brit struggled to muster the energy to crest the legendary summit, Porte fell back and willed his leader through the final kilometres. When Froome's around, Porte looks more than capable of assuming the top-dog status should the Brit fail—Porte climbs like a natural, unbowed by even the toughest mounts. And he's a neat time trial rider too.

But, he's been without pressure, and that may be the biggest doubt hanging over his career's future trajectory. Stepping from lieutenant to leader comes with it expectation, and new responsibilities—challenges that Porte has largely, even as he's been groomed, been shielded from. Concerning too has been his inconsistency, a troubling feature of his last two seasons. A handful of times in recent years there have been days in a Grand Tour where Porte's body just hasn't turned up. In 2014 this was explained by a bout of pneumonia, which understandably saw Porte crash out of overall contention after the race's first week. Whether that fragility will stick with him remains to be seen.

And then there's the ravenous Australian press pack that is eagerly pursuing a rider to take up the Evans torch. But even if that's been unhelpful, Evans' void can never be truly filled, the comparisons have been flattering for Porte as well. There's a confidence among many of his peers that he certainly has the class. The talent to make waves at the peak of the sport. It's just a matter of when.

An acid test for Porte's potential came in 2014 when the Australian was thrust into Team Sky's Tour de France leadership after Chris Froome withdrew through injury. Porte revelled in the position, moving himself into second overall, before cracking in the Alps with illness. His detractors were quick to poke holes in what that meant for Porte, but criticism came too quick, and drew conclusions unfair to Porte's character and physical ability. Porte had ridden away from many of the peloton's best on the awful rain-soaked cobbled stage to Arenberg, was out-climbed only by Sicilian Vincenzo Nibali, and then after succumbing to illness, bucked predictions he'd abandon by going on to finish.

It's Porte's fight that could be his strongest asset in the years to come, particularly now with his health being carefully managed and monitored by Team Sky's doctors.

Porte will spend the 2015 and 2016 seasons with Team Sky and, at 30, is entering his traditional prime as an endurance athlete. He's expected to split his attentions between the Giro d'Italia and Tour de France in the next few years.

LEANING INTO STAGE 9 OF THE 2014 TOUR

FEELING THE HEAT ON STAGE 10 OF THE 2014 TOUR

OUT IN FRONT ON STAGE 21 OF THE 2014 TOUR

Not very long ago, the notion that two Englishmen would follow an Australian on the Tour de France roll of honour would have defied common sense and all historical precedents. The five editions of the world's greatest race from 2010 to 2014 were, though, yet another stride in professional cycling's march towards globalisation—as well as a tentative step out of dark and scandal-ridden times.

Not every Tour was a classic, but they did all give us some fantastic stages. After an era dominated by the now disgraced Lance Armstrong and the stifling tactics of his US Postal team, finally the 'Grande Boucle' seemed to rediscover its capacity to shock as well as awe. The 2011 edition typified a riveting new age, with its labyrinthine plot and heart-stopping finale. The winner in that instance was the man who stayed calmest and most courageous while others were creating or falling victim to assorted dramas. He came from Australia and his name was Cadel Evans.

Bradley Wiggins' victory the following year rewarded a more prosaic performance, while Chris Froome's for the same Sky team in 2013 reflected his total dominance. Twelve months on from that, Vincenzo Nibali proved that crisis avoidance can be as much a prerequisite for a Tour champion as strength, speed and skill.

Out of the many highlights, it was hard to pick just five stages. Our final selection hopefully encapsulates a fraction of the suspense, excitement, beauty and heroism that make the Tour a sporting event like no other.

FIVE OF THE
BEST STAGES

2010 STAGE 15   2011 STAGE 19   2012 STAGE 11   2013 STAGE 13   2014 STAGE 5

DANIEL FRIEBE

2010, STAGE 15
PAMIERS TO BAGNÈRES-DE-LUCHON

WATCHING ANDY SCHLECK AND ALBERTO CONTADOR shadow-box for ownership of the race leader's yellow jersey in the second week of the 2010 Tour de France, some commentators would conclude that they didn't quite make rivalries like they used to.

'A pair of show ponies,' was the legendary former sprinter Mario Cipollini's verdict on a battle that made up for in suspense what it lacked in naked aggression.

Certainly, neither Schleck nor Contador seemed cut from the same creed as Tour champions and alpha males of yesteryear—the Eddy Merckxes, the Bernard Hinaults or the Lance Armstrongs. Fresh of face and mild of manner, Schleck juxtaposed remarkable talent with disconcerting naivety. Contador, meanwhile, hid the resolve that brought him back to racing after a brain aneurism early in his career beneath an unflappable, affable facade.

Entering the final week of the Tour, it was Schleck who had thus far prevailed, taking the yellow jersey off Cadel Evans on the second day in the Alps and keeping it until the morning of Stage 15. Finishing in Bagnères-de-Luchon, in the heart of the Pyrenees, and with the formidable Port de Balès climb peaking just 21km from home, this would be one of Contador's last chances to dethrone Schleck or at least loosen his crown before Paris.

Schleck led Contador by 31 seconds on general classification. As they meandered into the Barousse forest, at the foot of the Port de Balès climb, both men were safely cocooned in the peloton, poised to make their move. When the road clambered above the beech trees and onto the broad meadows

CONTADOR IN THE YELLOW JERSEY

VOECKLER WINS THE STAGE

of Mont Né, the gradient eased slightly but the drama reached its climax: just over a kilometre from the pass, Schleck kicked hard on the pedals and began to draw away from the group containing Contador. Then, catastrophe: his chain derailed and with it his momentum.

Professional cycling's unwritten moral code said that Contador should now have waited. Instead, he blew past his stricken rival with an attack of his own. Half an hour later, after a heart-stopping descent, Contador swept over the finish-line in Bagnères-de-Luchon nearly three minutes behind the breakaway stage winner Thomas Voeckler, but thirty-nine seconds ahead of Schleck. The Spaniard now donned the yellow jersey amid catcalls from the crowd. 'I wasn't aware there was an incident. I planned to attack anyway,' he pleaded. Schleck was disgusted: after days of platitudes, he now seethed, 'My belly is full of anger'.

Schleck's father, Johnny, himself a former Tour rider, was also indignant. 'It's not the done thing, attacking when your rival has a problem like that. Andy is very down about the whole thing,' he grumbled the following morning.

Only over the next few weeks and months—long after Contador had issued an unconvincing video-taped apology the next day and gone on to win the Tour—did the full, tantalising subplot emerge. It transpired that, the night before the Port de Balès stage, Schleck's team-manager, Bjarne Riis, had secretly met Contador and agreed to a deal to make him Schleck's replacement in 2011. Then, two days later in Pau, Contador would eat the steak that he later blamed for a positive dope test resulting in his retrospective disqualification from the race. While it had been Contador standing on the top step of the podium in Paris, the history books would later record

that Schleck was the 2010 Tour de France champion.

Schleck ended up waiting a year and a half for justice to be done—not that this was how he viewed Contador's doping ban. 'I feel sad for Alberto, I have always believed in his innocence. The only positive is that there is finally a verdict after 566 days of uncertainty .... If now I am declared winner of the 2010 Tour de France it will not make me happy. I battled with Contador in that race and I lost. My goal is to win the Tour de France in a sporting way, being the best of all competitors, not in court.'

That was February 2012. Just over two years later, aged 29, Andy Schleck was retiring from professional cycling, a combination of injuries and dwindling motivation having doomed the ambition of adding to his 2010 victory on his own terms.

VOECKLER IN A BREAKAWAY BEFORE HIS WIN

SCHLECK CLIMBS WITH CONTADOR DURING THE SAME STAGE

2011, STAGE 19
MODANE TO L'ALPE D'HUEZ

THE TOUR DE FRANCE ROUTE DESIGNER, Thierry Gouvenou, glanced across at his boss and frowned. 'One hundred and nine kilometres and the finish on Alpe d'Huez!' Christian Prudhomme, the race director had just announced triumphantly. Was Gouvenou mishearing or misunderstanding something? A stage of the Tour de France—no less than what would probably be the race decider, the Alpine deathmatch—that would pack ascents of the Col du Galibier and Alpe d'Huez into just 109km? Gouvenou asked whether Prudhomme was sure, whether he wouldn't reconsider an idea they had first mooted the previous summer—the same route but with a double ascent of the Alpe, to bump up that distance. But Prudhomme shook his head. 'Short stage, plenty of drama.' The ringmaster of the Tour de France had made up his mind.

When it finally came, the day had a lot to live up to. To celebrate the hundredth anniversary of the Col du Galibier's first appearance on the route in 1911, Gouvenou and Prudhomme had already sent the peloton up the 2645-metre Alpine behemoth once, the previous afternoon. Andy Schleck had honoured it with a brilliant, audacious performance, attacking with 60km to go, on the Col d'Izoard, and clinging on to win on the summit of the Galibier. Back down the mountain, the surprise race leader, Thomas Voeckler, and Cadel Evans were no less heroic in limiting their losses.

Voeckler now led the Tour by 15 seconds from Andy Schleck, and just over a minute from Andy's brother, Frank, and Evans. Ahead of Prudhomme's bitesized blockbuster and second ascent of the Galibier in 24 hours, this time

CONTADOR STARTS TO BREAK AWAY

EVANS CONTINUES TO CLIMB ALPE D'HUEZ

SCHLECK ,CONTADOR AND SANCHEZ CLIMB

CONTADOR BREAKING AWAY

STAGE WINNER ROLLAND IS CHEERED BY FANS ON THE FINISH LINE

in the opposite direction, the battle for yellow could not have been more finely balanced.

Four riders could still conceivably win the Tour with just three days to go. Alberto Contador, the champion in 2007 and 2010 before his disqualification for doping, wasn't one of them. The Spaniard now tried to make amends, sensationally breaking clear after just 15km of Stage 20, on the lower slopes of the Col du Télégraphe. Andy Schleck followed him, as, initially, did Evans and Voeckler. The Australian and the Frenchman had both made grave mistakes, letting instinct overrule logic, but only Voeckler would pay the price: Evans was in fact saved by a mechanical problem, which forced him to drop back to the chasing peloton; Voeckler, meanwhile, floundered in no man's land, isolated between the Contador–Schleck tandem and the main bunch for what remained of the Télégraphe and most of the Galibier.

In the race director's car, Prudhomme chortled. Not even he could have foreseen such a spellbinding denouement. Consensus about who now looked the likeliest to stand atop the podium in Paris was shifting by the second, from Schleck to Evans and back again, and even—still—to Voeckler.

Finally, Voeckler's chances seemed to fade, then dissolve when Evans' group caught and then dropped him on the steep hairpins beneath the Galibier summit. Evans and Schleck senior then crested the pass 34 seconds after Contador and Schleck junior, and over a minute ahead of Voeckler. Andy was now *maillot jaune virtuel*—leader on the road. Evans, though, would have the following afternoon's individual time trial weighing heavily in his favour.

Before that, here on Stage 20, the Tour's most famous climb, Alpe d'Huez, reared menacingly out of the Oisans valley.

The Alpe throbbed under the weight and noise of half a million fans. Those camped on the first of the 21 hairpins would see Voeckler, Evans and Frank Schleck all reunited with Andy Schleck and Contador, having successfully chased and caught the pair on the long Galibier descent. But Contador was soon attacking again, and this time no one could follow. Voeckler, predictably, couldn't hold the wheels of even the Schlecks and Evans'.

France would get its winner— but only of the stage, not the Tour: Pierre Rolland, the 24-year-old *enfant prodige* of French cycling, had counter-attacked, reeled in and then passed Contador in the final kilometre.

Behind this duo, Evans again demonstrated all of his grit to finish fifth, flanked by the Schlecks. The younger of the siblings, Andy, would wear the yellow jersey in what was now practically a tie-breaker, the 42km penultimate-day time trial around Grenoble. But Evans, a far superior rider against the clock, duly overhauled his 57-second deficit, as expected: the final stage of the 2011 Tour in Paris was to serve as a mere procession, confirming the former mountain biker from the Northern Territory as the first Australian to win the Tour and the oldest champion, at 34, since World War Two.

A triumph of patience over panache, bravery over bravado, Evans had pieced together his Tour victory much in the same way as he had built his career. Stage 20 had typified his doggedness and made a 21st century classic out of an already spectacular 2011 Tour.

2012, STAGE 11
ALBERTVILLE TO LA TOUSSUIRE

CADEL EVANS WAS NOT GOING DOWN WITHOUT A FIGHT. The defending Tour de France champion began the 2012 race hopeful of making it two in a row, and on the first summit finish, to La Planche des Belles Filles, he almost took the stage win before Chris Froome pipped him on the line.

When the race reached the Alps, Evans was well placed, second overall to Bradley Wiggins, but almost two minutes down. Wiggins had crushed him—and everyone else—in the time trial on Stage 9, and there was still a time trial to come on the penultimate day. Evans knew that if he was going to beat Wiggins, he had to claim time in the mountains, where Wiggins was vulnerable.

It was a short but punishing stage, 148km, including the Col de la Madeleine, the Col du Glandon and Col la Croix de Fer, then the smaller Col du Mollard before the final ascent to the ugly ski station at La Toussuire, where Floyd Landis cracked and lost the yellow jersey in 2006.

It would surely come down to the final climb: it always did. Yet Evans had other ideas. On the Col du Glandon, 56km from the finish, the defending champion attacked. A sign of confidence or desperation? He had two BMC teammates in the break and they waited for him: it looked like a tactical masterstroke. But there was still a long way to go.

Behind, it was another Australian, Michael Rogers, who was dictating things in the chasing group. When Evans attacked, Rogers told Wiggins, his Team Sky leader, not to panic. The experienced Rogers was Sky's 'road captain'. He insisted that by maintaining a steady tempo they would gradually reel in Evans;

FANS CHEER ON THE PACK RIDING WITH THE OVERALL LEADERS

STAGE WINNER PIERRE ROLLAND

he reassured Wiggins that Evans would not be able to sustain his effort over the Col la Croix de Fer, Col du Mollard and La Toussuire.

He was right. Evans was caught and as they began the 18.5km climb to La Toussuire it became clear he was in trouble—perhaps his earlier move was born of desperation, after all. As Evans was dropped, his Tour defence over, it was Vincenzo Nibali, known as the Shark, who began inflicting pain, accelerating as the slope steepened. It seemed to put Wiggins in trouble, but also his teammate, Froome, who had been third overall at the start of the day.

Rogers was no longer with Wiggins, but Wiggins remembered his advice: steady does it; there was no need to react to every attack. Froome seemed to recover and led Wiggins back up to Nibali. If he had been flagging, Froome now had a second wind, because he went straight through the group, past Nibali, and attacked—and put Wiggins back in trouble.

With Froome forcing the pace, Wiggins, his head dropping and legs slowing, became detached. There was panic in the Team Sky car following this small group as they inched up the climb. 'Froomey, Froomey, Froomey. I'm hoping you've got the okay from Bradley for that?' the Sky directeur sportif, Sean Yates, said to Froome on the race radio.

'He was telling me that unless Brad explicitly said I could go, I would be having a spell in the naughty corner,' Froome would later write in his autobiography. 'I kept pushing. Then I heard Brad's voice on the radio. "NO-OOO, NO-OOO, NO-OOO." He sounded like a man who had just dropped his oxygen tank near the top of Everest. Brad was folding physically and mentally, and quicker than I had thought possible.'

Froome eased up and looked round. 'I slowed and waited for him. He hadn't just cracked; I think he felt betrayed.'

Wiggins and Froome arrived at the summit of La Toussuire together, almost a minute behind the stage winner, Pierre Rolland. While Wiggins was ushered away to the podium to be presented with the yellow jersey, Froome was swamped by journalists. 'He asked me to slow down so I waited for him,' he said.

Told he could win the Tour, Froome said: 'Maybe one day ... I think Bradley's in a better position to win the Tour this year than I am, to be honest. I'll follow orders at all costs. I'm part of a team and I have to do what the team asks me to do.'

An uneasy truce descended between Froome and Wiggins for the rest of the Tour, but tension bubbled below the surface—and spilled out in later accounts, with Wiggins revealing that he felt so let down by Froome that he almost quit the race the night they reached La Toussuire.

It was an incident that defined the 2012 Tour but left us with more questions than answers. Was Froome attacking to try and win? And although Wiggins went on to become the first British winner, might Froome have beaten him to it if they had been on opposing teams? Froome believed so, and a year later, with Wiggins sidelined with injury, he proved he had what it took, becoming the second British winner.

FANS DRESSED AS SKIERS CHEER LEADERS, BRADLEY WIGGINS AND CHRISTOPHER FROOME

LEIPHEIMER RIDES IN A BREAKAWAY

VOECKLER RIDES IN THE BEST CLIMBER'S POLKA-DOT JERSEY

2013, STAGE 13
TOURS TO SAINT-AMAND-MONTROND

STAGE 13 OF THE 2013 TOUR DE FRANCE looked, on paper, to be one of those listless, uneventful days when even the most assiduous armchair spectators can safely detach themselves from the sofa, perhaps put up a deckchair or mow the lawn.

That was on paper. On the road what ended up unfolding across the plains of the Indre-et-Loire département was one of the most relentlessly compelling Tour stages in recent memory. It was indeed, as the winner, Mark Cavendish, reflected later, a day that fans of cycling would remember and rhapsodise about for decades.

The Tour had not been going well for Cavendish. A winner of 24 stages in the previous five editions, the Manxman had mustered a single victory in the first ten days of the 2013 race, as the route tacked southeast across France's central bread-basket and towards the Alps. Even more than by his three defeats in bunch gallops to his new nemesis, Marcel Kittel, Cavendish felt bruised and bedevilled by misfortune.

Crashes, broken bikes and poor form had already sapped his resolve before a second defeat to his new nemesis, Marcel Kittel, and an unseemly tangle with German team-mate, Tom Veelers, in the stampede to the line on Stage 10 to Saint-Malo. The following day, roadside 'fans' would let Cavendish know exactly who they felt was to blame when he arrived on the start-ramp for his Stage 11 time trial to Mont-St Michel. The boos and jeers didn't stop until he crossed the finish-line. Worse, much worse, was the drizzle of urine that came from the plastic bottle of one Veelers sympathiser.

FROOME RIDING IN THE PACK

CONTADOR WITH HIS TEAMMATES

VALVERDE RIDING WITH HIS TEAM

CAVENDISH CELEBRATING AFTER CROSSING THE FINISH LINE

Kittel beat Cavendish again on Stage 12, and the trend indicated that similar terrain would yield a similar outcome the following day. In cycling, though, there is one factor that can turn even the flattest, most innocuous course into a snarling gauntlet run: the weather, or more precisely, the breeze. Often it doesn't need much—just enough to make the sunflowers sway—if the angles are right and the road exposed.

As experienced and canny in the wind as seasoned yachtsmen, Cavendish's Belgian-based Omega Pharma-Quick Step team were among the likeliest candidates to make pandemonium happen. Their directeur sportif, Wilfried Peeters, had flagged down his counterpart from the Dutch Belkin outfit, Nico Verhoeven, in a hotel carpark before the stage start. 'If we want fireworks, will you help us light them?' Peeters had asked him, or words to that effect. Verhoeven had nodded.

The cue came after 56km, in Nouans-Les-Fontaines, when Peeters barked his instructions over the intercom radio. With gusts now coming from the side, the Omega riders, Tony Martin and Michal

Kwiatkowski, swung towards the middle of the road, accelerated and unleashed mayhem on the peloton behind. It was an old trick but a devastating one: by moving out of the gutter and towards the centre-line, the riders leading the bunch had effectively halved the space in which those behind them could shelter in their slipstream. Some would simply run out of road, just as much as their legs and lungs deserted them. Crucially for Omega, Cavendish made it into the first group or echelon. A mechanical problem ensured that Marcel Kittel did not.

The Tour leader, Chris Froome of Team Sky, was tucked safely in among the leaders. Meanwhile, one of his rivals for overall glory, Alejandro Valverde, had dropped out of the front group due to a puncture with 90km to go. Trouble for Froome, though, was also brewing: Alberto Contador's Saxo-Tinkoff team-mates were the next to use the wind as their weapon, accelerating en masse with 32km to go and distancing Sky's *maillot jaune*.

Cavendish had ridden masterfully to follow Contador and Saxo-Tinkoff cavalry. Accustomed to sprinting

in a 200-strong peloton, he would make light work of leading home the fourteen-man group that had caused and survived the carnage. Froome trailed in just over a minute later. His advantage on the overall standings had been cut to two-and-a-half minutes.

Twenty-four hours earlier, a downcast Cavendish had mused that, at 28, 'maybe I'm just getting old.' Kittel's growing superiority, he said, perhaps reflected 'the cycle of life'.

In Saint-Amand Montrond just a day later he had claimed the most skilfully engineered and dramatic of his 25 Tour de France stage wins to date. Eddy Merckx's all-time record of 34 bouquets still looked a long way off, and another statistic still haunted him: in three seasons since Kittel turned professional, Cavendish still hadn't beaten the German in a head-to-head sprint.

What had at least been purged were the bitter memories of the previous few days. Stage 13 of the 2013 would take everyone privileged enough to witness it—and Mark Cavendish—a whole lot longer to forget.

2014, STAGE 5
YPRES TO ARENBERG PORTE DU HAINAUT

IT WAS THE ONE THEY ALL FEARED, and that was before the rain fell. A sense of foreboding hung heavy in the air in the centre of Ypres on the morning of 9 July 2014, before Stage 5 of the Tour de France.

The sombre mood was appropriate, given the historic significance of the town, and the proximity of the Grote Markt, where the team buses gathered, to the Menin Gate, a memorial to some of the thousands who died nearby in the First World War.

The Tour paid its respects on the 100th anniversary of the war, but the grim expressions on the faces of the riders had more to do with what lay ahead of them on a grey, overcast day. Cobbles, or *pavé*, and lots of it: seven sectors. Originally it was nine, but on the morning of the stage two were deemed too waterlogged, and therefore too dangerous, to venture over.

Still. The faces said it all. The defending champion, Chris Froome, looked not only miserable, but also fearful. He had crashed the previous day, hitting the road heavily and venturing tentatively out of his Team Sky bus wrapped in bandages.

It was a short stage, only 155.5km, but the riders knew it was likely to be decisive. Then, about 15 minutes before the start, the grey mist turned into heavy rain. Ahead of them lay 13km of cobbles, each section taking the riders over big, uneven stones: a bone-jarring, nerve-shredding experience. Most of the riders dreaded the next few hours, while others looked on the day as an opportunity. And to the cobbled specialists—Fabian Cancellara, Peter Sagan, Lars Boom, the Omega Pharma-Quick Step team—could be added a

CONTADOR CROSSES THE FINISH LINE

MOLLEMA DURING THE FIFTH STAGE

NIBALI WEARS THE YELLOW

SAGAN IN THE GREEN JERSEY CROSSES THE FINISH LINE

BOOM CELEBRATES CROSSING THE LINE

surprising name: Vincenzo Nibali and his Astana team.

Nibali was already in yellow, having won Stage 2 to Sheffield, but this was the stage the Sicilian had been targeting. The Italian had joined his teammates three days after Paris-Roubaix to get a feel for the cobbles and as he skimmed across the pavé his Dutch colleague, Lieuw Westra, was both surprised and impressed: 'Vincenzo is very good at descending and it's a little bit the same. His bike handling is very good. When we did the recce he rode very well over the cobblestones.'

Astana had a plan for the stage, and it saw Westra instigate the early move, which included other strong riders for this kind of stage—Australian Mat Hayman, world time trial champion Tony Martin, and Tony Gallopin. Froome's Tour, meanwhile, was over before they even reached the first cobbled section. The defending champion struggled to control his bike and hold his position in the rain and crashed twice, withdrawing in tears

after the second spill.

When they hit the cobbles, 87km into the stage, Westra was perfectly placed for Nibali, who was biding his time as Sagan's Cannondale team upped the pace on the approach to the treacherous Carrefour de l'Arbre. Then Belkin's Sep Vanmarcke strung out the front group until several favourites, including Alberto Contador and Alejandro Valverde, were distanced. Nibali, his Astana teammate Jakob Fuglsang and the young Polish rider, Michal Kwiatkowski, were all still there.

As the breakaway began to be swept up by the Belkin-led peloton they raced towards the final, critical sectors of pavé. The penultimate section, Wandignies-Hamage à Hornaing, was the longest, at 3.7km, and one of the most brutal. It was here that Westra, who had waited for his leader, went to the front, shadowed by Nibali and Fuglsang, and helped to force the most decisive split of the stage—perhaps of the entire Tour de France.

Kwiatkowski let a gap open and they were gone. Boom, spotting the danger, determined not to let all the good work done by his Belkin team go to waste, jumped across the gap. And on the very last section of pavé, at Wallers, Boom attacked. By now Westra had been dropped, but Nibali was unconcerned by Boom's acceleration—he had bigger ambitions than the stage win.

For Boom, though, it was perfect. The Dutchman arrived in Arenberg alone to claim his biggest ever win, nine years after the last Dutch stage victory. 'My plan was to jump away on the last sector, and that's how it worked out,' he said.

The day belonged to Boom, but also to Nibali and Astana, though Nibali acknowledged the fortune that always accompanies a good result on the cobbles. 'I almost crashed three times,' said the man who would eventually be crowned winner of the 2014 Tour. 'I was lucky, but we also got our tactics right.'

Published in 2015 by Hardie Grant Books

Hardie Grant Books (Australia)
Ground Floor, Building 1
658 Church Street
Richmond, Victoria 3121
www.hardiegrant.com.au

Hardie Grant Books (UK)
5th & 6th Floor
52–54 Southwark Street
London SE1 1RU
www.hardiegrant.co.uk

Cataloguing in publications data available from the National Library of Australia
Legends of the Tour
ISBN 978 1 74379 0489

Photographs: the publisher would like to thank Graham Watson
and Getty Images for photographs used throughout the book

Publisher: Pam Brewster
Cover and text design: Peter Daniel
Cover images courtesy of Graham Watson
Printed and bound in China by 1010 Printing International Limited